GREAT LIVES OBSERVED

Gerald Emanuel Stearn, *General Editor*

EACH VOLUME IN THE SERIES VIEWS THE CHARACTER AND ACHIEVEMENT OF A GREAT WORLD FIGURE IN THREE PERSPECTIVES—THROUGH HIS OWN WORDS, THROUGH THE OPINIONS OF HIS CONTEMPORARIES, AND THROUGH RETROSPECTIVE JUDGMENTS—THUS COMBINING THE INTIMACY OF AUTOBIOGRAPHY, THE IMMEDIACY OF EYEWITNESS OBSERVATION, AND THE OBJECTIVITY OF MODERN SCHOLARSHIP.

JOHN BRAEMAN, *editor of this volume in the Great Lives Observed series, is Professor of History at the University of Nebraska–Lincoln. He is the author of* Albert J. Beveridge: American Nationalist; *editor of* American Politics in the Twentieth Century; *and co-editor of* American Foreign Policy in the Twentieth Century, Change and Continuity in Twentieth-Century America: The 1920's, *and* Change and Continuity in Twentieth-Century America.

GREAT LIVES OBSERVED

WILSON

Edited by JOHN BRAEMAN

I cannot refrain from saying it: I am not one of those
who have the least anxiety
about the triumph of the principles I have stood for.
I have seen fools resist Providence before
and I have seen their destruction,
as will come upon these again
—utter destruction and contempt.
That we shall prevail is as sure as that God reigns.

—WOODROW WILSON
(Last public words, to a group
of people gathered outside his house
on Armistice Day, 1923)

A SPECTRUM BOOK

PRENTICE-HALL, INC., ENGLEWOOD CLIFFS, N.J.

Library of Congress Cataloging in Publication Data

BRAEMAN, JOHN.
  Wilson.

   (Great lives observed)   (A Spectrum book)
   Bibliography: p.
   1. Wilson, Woodrow, Pres. U. S., 1856–1924.
E767.B73   973.91′3′0924 [B]   72–7442
ISBN 0–13–960260–7
ISBN 0–13–960252–6 (pbk)

© 1972 by PRENTICE-HALL, INC.
Englewood Cliffs, New Jersey

A SPECTRUM BOOK

10 9 8 7 6 5 4 3 2 1

Printed in the United States of America

PRENTICE-HALL INTERNATIONAL, INC. (*London*)
PRENTICE-HALL OF AUSTRALIA, PTY. LTD. (*Sydney*)
PRENTICE-HALL OF CANADA, LTD. (*Toronto*)
PRENTICE-HALL OF INDIA PRIVATE LIMITED (*New Delhi*)
PRENTICE-HALL OF JAPAN, INC. (*Tokyo*)

Contents

PART ONE
WOODROW WILSON LOOKS AT THE WORLD

1
Scholar, Teacher, and University President   19

At Johns Hopkins, *19*   Student of American Political Institutions, *22*   Educational Reformer, *26*

2
The Road to the White House   31

The Political Conservative, *31*   Moving toward Progressivism, *33*   Governor of New Jersey, *40*   Campaigning for the Presidency, *42*

3
The Presidency   47

The New Freedom, *47*   Missionary Diplomacy, *56*   From Neutrality to War, *59*   A Just and Lasting Peace, *68*

PART TWO
WOODROW WILSON VIEWED BY HIS CONTEMPORARIES

4
The Man   83

5
Educational Reformer   90

v

vi

Introduction

Thomas Woodrow Wilson was born in Staunton, Virginia, December 28, 1856. His mother, Janet (called Jessie) Woodrow, was the daughter of a Scottish Presbyterian minister who had settled in Ohio. His paternal grandfather, James Wilson, had migrated from Ulster in the early eighteenth century. His father, Joseph Ruggles Wilson, himself a Presbyterian minister, had been brought up in Ohio but had moved to Virginia in 1853. When Wilson was two, the family moved to Augusta, Georgia. In 1870, his father became minister of the First Presbyterian Church and a professor in the theological seminary at Columbia, South Carolina. Four years later he took a pastorate at Wilmington, North Carolina. Young Woodrow (as he would later call himself) was extremely close to and strongly influenced, even dominated, by his father, imbibing from him his deep and unquestioning religious faith, his admiration for the English literary classics, and his dedication to intellectual and moral ideals. Dr. Wilson was an exacting taskmaster, whose demands fired the boy's ambitions to make his mark as a statesman but left him with a haunting sense of personal inadequacy that doomed him to perpetual self-disappointment. Having grown up in the South during the grim post–Civil War years, Wilson retained throughout his life a sympathy for and an understanding of his native region.

After attending Davidson College in North Carolina in 1873–74, he transferred in the autumn of 1875 to the College of New Jersey (Princeton). He did not shine as a student in his formal classroom work, but he won a reputation as an effective debater, read widely in the lives of the great British statesmen, and began his lifelong interest in government and public affairs, writing in his senior year an essay entitled "Cabinet Government in the United States" that was published in the August, 1879, issue of the *International Review*. After his graduation from Princeton in 1879, Wilson, avid for a career in public affairs, entered the law school at the University of Virginia to study for the bar. But poor health forced his return to Wilmington. After continuing his studies at home, he moved to Atlanta, Georgia, in 1882 and was admitted to the bar there. But he failed to prosper as a lawyer because of his shyness, his disdain for mere money-grubbing, and his revulsion at the intellectual narrowness and pettiness of routine legal practice. In the autumn of 1883, despite lingering regrets about giving up his political dreams, he abandoned the law and entered upon graduate study at Johns Hopkins University. Though repelled by the German-inspired emphasis upon specialized research he found at Hopkins, his elaboration of his Princeton senior essay, published in the *Overland Monthly* of January, 1884, as "Committee or Cabinet Government," won for him a fellowship in the history department, and he was awarded his Ph.D. in June, 1886. His thesis, *Congressional Government: A Study in American Politics,* published in January, 1885, was probably his most important scholarly work. The study was a landmark analysis of American political practice that, reflecting his long-standing admiration for the British system of responsible parliamentary government, emphasized the evils growing out of the separation of the legislative and executive branches of the government and the resulting diffusion and fragmentation of power in congressional committees.

While practicing law in Atlanta, Wilson had fallen in love with Ellen Louise Axson, the daughter of a Presbyterian minister in Rome, Georgia; and they were married on June 24, 1885. The couple had three daughters: Margaret, Jessie Woodrow, and Eleanor Randolph. A remarkable woman, Eleanor Axson was, next to Wilson's father, the single most important influence in his life, providing him with the emotional support and sympathy he so badly needed. Her death on August 6, 1914, during the European war crisis, was a severe blow to Wilson. Heavily dependent upon feminine encouragement and understanding, he married Edith Bolling Galt on December 18, 1915.

Wilson taught history at Bryn Mawr College from 1885 to 1888, then went to Wesleyan University as professor of history and political economy, and in 1890 was appointed professor of jurisprudence and political economy at Princeton. His wide reading, infectious enthusiasm, painstaking devotion to clarity of expression, and sure grasp of the apt phrase made him a highly popular undergraduate teacher. At the same time, he was a prolific writer. His more important scholarly works during this period were *The State:*

Elements of Historical and Political Practice (1889), a comparative survey of the history and development of political institutions; *Division and Reunion, 1829–1889* (1893), a brief survey of American history from the Jacksonian era through Reconstruction; a biography, *George Washington* (1896); the five-volume *History of the American People* (1902); and a series of lectures at Columbia University, *Constitutional Government in the United States* (1908). As a political scientist, Wilson was a pioneer in the application of evolutionary and pragmatic approaches to the study of American political institutions. But his historical writings are marred by thin research, lack of originality, and a deeply conservative attitude toward economic and social change.

A leader of the reform-minded younger faculty, Wilson was unanimously chosen president of Princeton in 1902. As president, Wilson wished to emphasize the intellectual objectives of the university and to subordinate the popular athletic and social "side shows." He raised admission standards and, in line with his commitment to the ideal of liberal culture, he revised the curriculum with the aim of turning out well-rounded, broadly educated gentlemen rather than narrow specialists. Growing dubious about the worth of the lecture system as an effective means of intellectual stimulation, he appointed to the faculty in 1905 forty-seven "preceptors," young scholars whose primary responsibility would be individually supervising students and running small discussion groups. But his effort to replace undergraduate eating clubs with colleges where students and younger faculty would have an opportunity for continuous interaction (the so-called quadrangle plan) roused the strong—and successful—opposition of many alumni and older faculty. An even more disappointing setback was the defeat of his plan to make the graduate school the intellectual center of the university by placing it at the physical center. Although his primary motivation was his ambition to make Princeton a unified community dedicated to the life of the mind, as time went on Wilson came more and more to picture the struggle as a contest of democracy versus special privilege.

During these years, Wilson belonged to the Grover Cleveland–sound money wing of the Democratic party. Though not a doctrinaire advocate of laissez-faire, he had no sympathy with the agrarian revolt of the 1890s, thought labor unions un-American, and remained suspicious of government regulation of business. As his lecturing and activities at Princeton brought him into increasing prominence, the leaders of the conservative, anti-Bryan wing of the Democratic party—such as Colonel George Harvey, the editor of *Harper's Weekly* and a business associate of J. P. Morgan—began to look upon him as possible presidential timber. In 1910 Harvey persuaded ex-Senator James S. Smith, Jr., the Democratic boss of New Jersey, to offer Wilson the party's gubernatorial nomination. Wilson, bitterly disappointed over the defeat of his graduate school plan, grasped the opportunity as a face-saving device to extricate him from his Princeton difficulties. At first, the reformers within both parties looked suspiciously upon Wilson as the hand-picked tool of the machine. But his eloquent espousal of progressive principles in his campaign won most over to his support. Riding the high tide of reform sentiment in New Jersey, he was elected governor by a large majority.

Immediately after the election came the first test of Wilson's newfound commitment to reform. With the Democrats having unexpectedly won a majority in the legislature, party boss Jim Smith decided that he wanted to return to the Senate. But under pressure from his liberal supporters, who reminded him of his advocacy of the principle of popular election of senators in the campaign, Wilson came out publicly against Smith and successfully threw his influence behind the selection of the undistinguished Bryan admirer James E. Martine, who had run unopposed in the Democratic senatorial preference primary. He then pushed through the legislature a far-reaching program of reform—including the direct primary, an effective public utilities commission, a corrupt-practices act, a workmen's compensation law, and legislation permitting New Jersey's cities to adopt the commission form of government. In 1911, the Republicans, thanks to the knifing of the Democratic ticket by the Smith machine in Essex County, recaptured control of both houses of the legislature, thus temporarily stymying Wilson's proposals for more stringent regulation of corporations. But after the election of 1912, Wilson won adoption of his so-called Seven Sisters laws, prohibiting mergers that promoted monopoly and preventing the future formation of holding companies within the state.

Wilson's achievements as governor of New Jersey brought him

into increasing national prominence as the possible Democratic presidential nominee in 1912—this time as the hope of the progressive wing of the party. His new stance led to a break with such former boosters as Colonel Harvey. And when the publication of his earlier adverse comments about William Jennings Bryan threatened to derail his candidacy, he succeeded in making his peace with the Great Commoner. Although Champ Clark of Missouri, the Speaker of the House of Representatives, led on the early ballots, an alliance between the Wilson forces and the supporters of Congressman Oscar W. Underwood of Alabama denied Clark the required two-thirds majority. Wilson then went on to win the nomination on the forty-sixth ballot.

Influenced by the advice of Boston reformer Louis D. Brandeis, Wilson made his "New Freedom"—with its pledge to free the nation from the grip of monopoly and restore competition—the keystone of his campaign. His attitude toward social welfare legislation, while more positive than many writers have assumed, remained sufficiently ambivalent that the majority of its champions supported Theodore Roosevelt's Progressive party. Thanks to the split within GOP ranks, Wilson won a decisive majority in the electoral college despite his polling only 42 percent of the popular vote, while the Democrats won control of both houses of Congress.

After his election, Wilson moved boldly and energetically to utilize the full powers inherent in the presidency to lead his party in Congress and to carry out his campaign promises to destroy the system of special privilege instituted by the Republicans and to open up avenues of opportunity for the ambitious and enterprising "little man" on the make. Taking as his first target the tariff, he effectively mobilized public opinion to push through Congress in October, 1913, the Underwood bill reducing the average tariff rates from about 40 percent to approximately 26 percent and imposing a graduated income tax. Next turning to reform of the banking and currency system in order to break the grip of Wall Street upon the country's credit resources, he successfully reconciled the differences within the Democratic ranks in Congress and overcame the hostility of the nation's leading bankers to gain adoption of the Federal Reserve Act in December, 1913. The new law established a decentralized system of twelve Federal Reserve Banks to act as central banks for their regions, combined private ownership and control of the district Reserve Banks with government supervision at the top through a presidentially appointed Federal Reserve Board, and provided for an elastic yet sound currency.

At first, Wilson's favored solution to the trust problem—embodied in the Clayton bill—was to amend the Sherman antitrust law to define in detail unfair trade practices and then rely upon the courts for enforcement. Again influenced by Brandeis, however, he switched to an approach more in accord with TR's New Nationalist ideas: the prohibition in general and sweeping terms of unfair trade practices with the establishment of a Federal Trade Commission empowered to exercise continuous supervision over businesses and to issue cease-and-desist orders to violators. The Federal Trade Commission Act was approved by Congress in September, 1914. But as a result, the Clayton bill, now left adrift by the president, was watered down in the Senate before its final adoption the following month.

With the passage of these measures, Wilson thought that the program of reform envisaged in his New Freedom program had been completed. His determination to slow down was reinforced by the business slump in 1914. Thus, despite his campaign talk about breaking up the trusts, he shied from any massive antitrust campaign, while most of his appointees to the new regulatory agencies were satisfactory to the business community. Although he was persuaded by the personal appeal of Andrew Furuseth, the president of the Seamen's Union, to approve the La Follette Seamen's Act of 1915 improving the lot of the nation's sailors, his continued adherence to the New Freedom doctrine of "special privileges to none," reinforced by his traditional Democratic states' rights principles, led him to resent adamantly the American Federation of Labor's demand for exemption of unions from the antitrust laws, to oppose a federal system of agricultural credits, and to withhold his support from the proposed national child-labor law and the woman's suffrage amendment to the Constitution.

But the Republican gains in the 1914 congressional elections, the rapid disintegration of the Progressive party, and the growing likelihood of Theodore Roosevelt's return to the GOP in 1916 led him to move to the left in hopes of winning the support of advanced Progressives. The first sign of his new departure was his appointment in January, 1916, of Brandeis to the Supreme Court despite bitter opposition even within his own party. Next he threw his weight behind passage of the Federal Farm Loan Act, setting up a federally financed system of Farm Loan Banks to provide low-interest mortgages to farmers; the Kern-McGillicuddy bill, a model workmen's compensation law for federal employees; and the Keating-Owen bill, prohibiting the shipment in interstate commerce of goods manufactured in whole or in part by children under fourteen years of age. Then, faced with the threat of a nationwide railroad strike on the eve of elections, he pushed through Congress in September, 1916, the Adamson Act granting interstate railroad workers the eight-hour workday. As a result, Wilson could boast in his speech accepting the Democratic party's presidential nomination in 1916 that his administration had enacted into law most of the 1912 Progressive party platform. And his new departure brought its hoped-for reward when a large number of former Progressives rallied to his standard in the 1916 election.

Given Wilson's lack of interest and experience in foreign affairs before his election to the presidency, it is ironical that Wilson faced his most difficult problems in the realm of foreign policy. Despite his temporary enthusiasm in the aftermath of the Spanish-American War for American overseas expansion, he entered the White House as the champion of a new American diplomacy that would place the good of mankind above the selfish interests of the United States. Thus, as one of his first acts after becoming president, he withdrew the administration's support for participation by American bankers in the proposed six-power consortium to finance Chinese railroad development, on the ground that the conditions of the loan impaired Chinese sovereignty. Unfortunately, this moralistic approach ignored Far Eastern realities, and the resulting collapse of the consortium left the Chinese even more at the mercy of the Japanese. On the other hand, the United States did forcefully—and successfully—protest in 1915 Japan's Twenty-One Demands as a threat to China's political and territorial integrity. And despite the ambiguous Lansing-Ishii Agreement of 1917 recognizing Japan's "special interests" in China, the United States remained the major barrier to Japanese expansionist aims.

The limitations of Wilson's moralistic approach to foreign affairs was most strikingly revealed in what Arthur S. Link has aptly termed his "missionary diplomacy" toward Latin America. Despite

Wilson's disavowal of the Taft administration's "dollar diplomacy," his own commitment to preserving American supremacy in Central America and the Caribbean in order to protect the Panama Canal, coupled with his ambition to teach the Latin Americans "to elect good men," led the United States into a deepening morass of involvement and interference highlighted by military intervention in the Dominican Republic and Haiti. Wilson's most serious difficulties were with Mexico. His determination to topple Mexican dictator Victoriano Huerta—though successful in its immediate aim —brought the two nations to the verge of war and culminated in the unhappy Pershing punitive expedition of 1916–17.

But Wilson's most explosive foreign policy problem grew out of the outbreak of war in Europe in August, 1914. Immediately after the outbreak of hostilities, Wilson urged the American people to remain neutral in thought as well as deed. Unfortunately, the policies followed by his administration proved distinctly more favorable to the Allies than to the Central Powers. Although he was deeply aggrieved at British violations of neutral rights, his own anglophile sympathies, the pro-Allied bias of the public at large, the vital importance of Allied war purchases to the American economy, and the fear of antagonizing Britain in the face of this country's worsening relations with Germany led Wilson to acquiesce in the British maritime system and to leave the question of compensation to future negotiation. In striking contrast was his adamant stand against German submarine warfare. Drawing a distinction between the British interference with property rights and Germany's destruction of lives, he warned on February 10, 1915, that the United States would hold Germany to "strict accountability" for the sinking of American vessels or the loss of American lives.

The first crisis came over the sinking of the British liner *Lusitania* on May, 1915, with the loss of over a thousand lives, including 128 Americans. Himself deeply shocked by the inhumanity of the attack—and pressured by the popular outcry—Wilson demanded that Germany abandon its unrestricted submarine warfare and, in a virtual ultimatum, warned that the repetition of such action would be regarded as "deliberately unfriendly." Although Secretary of State William Jennings Bryan, fearful that Wilson's stand would involve the United States in war with Germany, resigned in June rather than sign the second *Lusitania* note, Wilson won a major diplomatic triumph when following the sinking of the British steamer *Arabic* in August, 1915, with the loss of two American lives, the German government pledged not to sink "liners" without warning and without making provision for the safety of the passengers. But having thus committed the United States to this policy of holding Germany to "strict accountability" regarding submarine warfare, Wilson henceforth felt that he could not back down without disastrously destroying the country's prestige. Thus, when Democratic insurgents in Congress pushed in March, 1916, for adoption of the Gore-McLemore resolutions warning Americans not to travel on belligerent ships, Wilson refused to yield on the right of Americans to travel freely on the high seas and intervened decisively to secure the tabling of the resolutions.

Wilson's stand against German submarine warfare spurred bitter denunciations from German-American groups. At the same time, pro-Allied enthusiasts led by Theodore Roosevelt assailed him for not taking an even stronger line toward Germany. And this group launched a major attack upon the administration for its alleged failure to prepare the country militarily. But Wilson undercut the preparedness advocates by putting forth his own preparedness program in late 1915. And his threat to break diplomatic relations following the sinking of the French cross-channel packet *Sussex* on May 24, 1916, forced the German government to promise to abandon its unrestricted submarine warfare entirely. Although the German promise was conditioned upon this country's compelling the British to respect the rules of international law, the easing of United States–German tensions following this so-called *Sussex* pledge gave the Democrats their winning slogan, "He has kept us out of war," in the 1916 election.

But no one understood better than Wilson himself how precarious continued peace was, depending as it did upon Germany's adherence to its *Sussex* pledge. The only way out of the dilemma appeared to be to bring the war to a swift end. Wilson's determination to act as a mediator was strengthened by his conviction that the United States was the only great power sufficiently disinterested to bring about a just settlement. Since the early autumn of 1914 he had been exploring without success the possibility of effective mediation. He even approved the House-Grey memorandum of February, 1915, that "on hearing from Britain and France that the time was opportune" he would summon a peace conference and that if Germany proved unyielding the United States "would probably enter the war against Germany." But the Allies, aware of the constitutional limitations on the American chief executive, perhaps sensing Wilson's own continued ambivalence, and still hopeful of victory, failed to follow through. Immediately after his election, Wilson, encouraged by German peace overtures and increasingly disillusioned with the Allies, made a last-ditch effort at mediation. And on January 22, 1917, he laid down in a speech before the Senate his plan for a lasting peace, "a peace without victory."

After more than two years of bloody war, however, neither side was willing to accept such a peace. Although Wilson perhaps could have forced the Allies into line by economic pressure, the German leaders no longer had any confidence in the American chief executive. Yielding to the demands of the military, the German government announced on February 1, 1917, the resumption of unrestricted submarine warfare against all shipping, belligerent and neutral, in the hope of winning a swift victory. Although Wilson immediately broke diplomatic relations with Germany, he continued to hope against hope that American entrance into the war could be avoided. For a time he leaned toward simply following the policy of armed neutrality. But the practical difficulties involved, the refusal of the German government to make concessions, his own renewed belief following the First Russian Revolution that the war was a struggle between the autocracies and the democracies, the publication of the Zimmermann note suggesting a German-Mexican alliance against the United States, the sinking of American ships, and the growing popular outcry led Wilson to ask Congress on April 2, 1917, for a declaration of war. In his agony, he transformed the issue from the defense of American neutral rights into a crusade to make the world "safe for democracy."

The war brought to the United States an unprecedented concentration of power in Washington. The nation's youth were drafted into the army. The federal government took over the nation's railroads, telephone and telegraph companies, and shipping and ship building. Food and fuel controls were imposed. The War Industries Board directed and coordinated production. The administration threw its support behind organized labor's demands for union recognition, higher wages, and even the eight-hour workday in return for a no-strike pledge. New and higher taxes were levied upon large incomes, profits, and inheritances in order to finance the war effort. Not only was the United States successfully transformed into the arsenal of money, materials, and weapons for the Allies, but, to the surprise of friend and foe, the American Expeditionary Force was ready for the front at a decisive moment in the war. There was also a less positive side to America's wartime experience. The propaganda activities of the administration's Committee on Public Information, headed by George Creel, spurred wartime hysteria and vigilantism against all things German, while the federal government—at times at Wilson's personal instigation—barred the mails to radical publications and imprisoned critics of the war such as Socialist leader Eugene V. Debs under the Espionage and Sedition acts.

After the victorious Bolsheviks in Russia published the embarrassing secret treaties among the Allies, Wilson was moved to set forth his own war aims in order to undercut the Bolshevik attacks on the war as an imperialist struggle, to undermine the morale of the Central Powers, and to justify the war to liberals at home and abroad and, perhaps most importantly, to himself. In a speech before Congress on January 8, 1918, he set forth his famous Fourteen Points as the basis not only for a just and lasting peace, but for a new world order resting upon "a general association of nations" guaranteeing "political independence and territorial integrity to great and small states alike." With American supplies and troops having turned the tide on the battlefield, the Germans in October, 1918, appealed to Wilson for peace on the basis of the Fourteen Points. Wilson's refusal to deal with "the military masters of the monarchical autocrats of Germany" hastened the revolution that overthrew the Hohenzollern regime. And in face of Wilson's threat to make a separate peace, the Allies grudgingly accepted the Fourteen Points in principle, although with two vital reservations—the British insisting upon reserving the question of freedom of the seas for later discussion, and the French demanding reparations from Germany for war damages to the civilian population.

At the seeming height of his influence, Wilson decided to go in person to the peace conference to insure the triumph of his plans.

But despite his tremendous worldwide prestige, Wilson faced immense—and perhaps insuperable—obstacles to the fulfillment of his dreams. Some were of his own making. By going to Paris he lost his unique position above the battle, while depriving the country of badly needed leadership at home. His idealistic peace goals conflicted with the secret treaties made by the Allies, and though Wilson, contrary to what he later claimed, knew of their existence, he had not made full American participation in the war conditional upon their abrogation. Nor did he successfully exploit the leverage given him by the immense Allied war debts to force the Allied representatives into line at the conference. In October, 1918, he had publicly appealed for the election of a Democratic Congress as a vote of personal confidence. But war-bred resentments against the "ins," midwestern anger over the price ceilings imposed upon wheat but not cotton, and the successful reunification of the GOP resulted in Republican majorities in both houses. This seeming repudiation weakened Wilson's influence abroad, while placing control of the crucial Senate Foreign Relations Committee in hostile hands. And he aggravated the situation by his failure to include on the American peace commission any senator or prominent Republican.

But many of Wilson's difficulties were beyond his control. Russia was in the midst of revolutionary upheaval, Central Europe was in chaos, and the specter of bolshevism haunted the rest of Europe, leading to a demand for a quick settlement, any settlement regardless of terms. The legacy of wartime passions—even in the United States—spurred loud demands for harsh treatment of Germany. The principle of national self-determination was easier to enunciate than to implement, given the tangled map of Central Europe. Fearful that the break-up of the conference would have cataclysmic effects upon the existing European political structure—and obsessed with the need to win the approval of the great powers for the inclusion of his proposed League of Nations in the peace treaty—Wilson found himself forced repeatedly to compromise.

The principle of hands-off of Russia was abandoned even before the conference met, as Wilson, after first hesitating, joined the Allies in military intervention against the Bolsheviks. The confused situation in Russia coupled with French hostility to the Bolshevik regime meant that Russia was not even represented at the conference. Germany's colonies were in every case awarded to that Allied power that had seized them during the war or that had been promised them by the secret treaties. Wilson even had to yield on Japan's taking over Germany's rights in Shantung. Freedom of the seas was not mentioned, nor was anything done to foster freer trade or promote disarmament. Wilson had to agree to French occupation of the Rhineland and the Saar and to keep Germany out of the League of Nations, while Germany was forced to sign a blank check on future reparations and admit its sole guilt for starting the war.

But without Wilson's efforts, the results would have been far less liberal. He prevented the permanent separation of the Rhineland from Germany and the French annexation of the Saar. The former German colonies were granted, not as outright colonial possessions, but as mandates under the League of Nations. Despite the shortcomings of the territorial settlements, the map of Europe was redrawn in closer approximation to the principle of nationality than ever before. Above all, Wilson gained the approval of the powers for his cherished League of Nations. Although unhappy over the departures from the Fourteen Points he had been forced to approve, Wilson hoped that the League would provide the means for the peaceful readjustment of the treaty's worst shortcomings.

At first American public opinion was highly favorable to the treaty. Even Senator Henry Cabot Lodge of Massachusetts, the powerful chairman of the Senate Foreign Relations Committee, though insistent upon reservations to define more explicitly American obligations under the League and to assure Congress final say in the fulfillment of those obligations, was not opposed in principle to the treaty and the League. But a heterogeneous opposition composed of American nationalists fearful of any surrender of American sovereignty, Republicans seeking party advantage, disillusioned liberals who saw the League as a futile attempt to uphold an unjust peace, and ethnic groups such as the Irish-Americans, German-Americans, and Italian-Americans disappointed by the treatment accorded their homelands by the treaty, gained steadily in strength with the passage of time. Even so, had Wilson proved more conciliatory, he probably could have won over enough moderates to gain Senate approval of the League covenant with its essentials unimpaired. But he would not yield an inch.

Hoping to appeal to the country over the head of the Senate, Wilson set out on September 3, 1919, on a cross-country tour. Physically and emotionally exhausted, he collapsed after speaking at Pueblo, Colorado, on September 25, and had to be rushed back to Washington. On October 2, he suffered a stroke that left him partially paralyzed. Although he slowly recovered, he no longer had the physical and emotional strength to provide the country with effective leadership. His resulting isolation from political realities made him even more inflexible—and his stubbornness and inflexibility was perhaps further aggravated by the brain damage resulting from his stroke. So despite pleas from all sides that he compromise, he remained adamant. At the final showdown in March, 1920, enough Democrats followed his orders to vote against the treaty with the Lodge reservations to block ratification of the League once and for all.

Because of his preoccupation with the League fight, his physical breakdown, and the limitations of his progressivism, Wilson failed to deal with the manifold domestic problems facing the country after the war. The elaborate wartime structure of controls was dismantled as quickly as possible. The railroads, telephone and telegraph companies, and merchant marine were returned to private hands on terms favorable to business. War contracts were abruptly terminated; the army was demobilized in helter-skelter fashion; and the federal government undertook no program of public works to ease the transition to peace. When organized labor went out in a series of strikes during 1919 in reaction to the rapidly increasing price level, the Wilson administration threw its weight against the strikers. Bereft of leadership from Washington, the country slid into a serious depression starting in the summer of 1920. And the continuing wartime passions, the xenophobia spurred by Wilson's attacks on the divided loyalties of the foreign born during the 1916 elections and the fight over the Versailles treaty, the fear of radicalism aroused by the Bolshevik Revolution and the wave of strikes in 1919, and the political ambitions of Wilson's attorney general, A. Mitchell Palmer, combined to produce the notorious "Red Scare" of 1919–20.

Despite his broken health, Wilson hoped to make the 1920 election a "solemn referendum" on the League and even harbored ambitions of running for reelection. But it was not to be. The hard-headed Democratic politicians would not hear of his renomination. Both the Democratic and Republican presidential nominees, James M. Cox and Warren G. Harding, took ambiguous stands on the League. And the accumulated popular resentments against the "ins" swept Harding and the Republicans to a landslide victory. Wilson's last months in the White House were spent in gloomy and depressing waiting. After leaving office, he lived on in Washington for nearly three more years, lonely and embittered, in steadily worsening health. Although he maintained a dignified silence on political questions, he continued to dream of possibly running for the presidency again in 1924. And to the last he remained confident in his faith that the principles for which he had stood would ultimately triumph. He died in his sleep the morning of February 3, 1924.

Chronology of the Life of Woodrow Wilson

1856	(December 28) Born in Staunton, Virginia, the son of the Reverend Joseph Ruggles Wilson and Janet (Jessie) Woodrow.
1873–74	Attends Davidson College.
1875	Transfers to the College of New Jersey (Princeton).
1879	Publishes first major article.
	Graduates from Princeton and enters University of Virginia Law School.
1882	Begins law practice in Atlanta, Georgia.
1883	Begins graduate study at Johns Hopkins University.
1885	Publishes *Congressional Government*.
	Marries Ellen Louise Axson and begins teaching at Bryn Mawr College.
1886	Receives Ph.D.
1888–90	Teaches at Wesleyan University.
1890–1902	Teaches at Princeton.
1902–10	President of Princeton.
1910	Elected governor of New Jersey.
1912	Elected president of the United States.
1913–14	Secures adoption of Underwood tariff, Federal Reserve, Federal Trade Commission, and Clayton antitrust laws. Intervenes in Mexico to oust Huerta.
1914	Proclaims American neutrality in World War.
	Death of first wife.
1915	Holds Germany to strict accountability on submarine warfare.
	Launches preparedness program.
	Marries Edith Bolling Galt.
1916	Moves to left in domestic policy to win support of advanced progressives.
	Forces Germany to abandon its unrestricted submarine warfare.
	Endorses League of Nations idea.
	Orders Pershing punitive expedition into Mexico.
	Reelected president on peace and progressivism issues.
	Undertakes last-ditch mediation effort to end war.

1917	Asks Congress to declare war.
1917–18	Mobilizes nation for war effort.
1918	Sets forth war aims in Fourteen Points address.
	Unsuccessfully appeals for election of Democratic Congress.
	Arranges armistice.
	Leaves for Paris Peace Conference.
1919	Wins approval of the powers for the League of Nations.
	Signs Versailles treaty.
	Appeals to country on the League.
	Suffers stroke.
	Refuses to compromise on reservations to treaty; Senate rejects treaty with and without the Lodge reservations.
1919–20	Provides no leadership in domestic affairs in aftermath of war.
1920	Remains adamant against compromise on the League; Senate rejects for second and final time treaty with Lodge reservations.
	Hopes blasted on running again and making election referendum on the League.
	Awarded Nobel Peace Prize.
1921–24	Lives in retirement in Washington, D.C.
	(February 3, 1924) dies.

WOODROW WILSON LOOKS AT THE WORLD

Wilson came to active politics relatively late in life. He spent the major part of his career as a scholar, teacher, and university president. But his success in politics following his nomination as governor of New Jersey in 1910 was meteoric. His championing of reform while governor brought him the presidential nomination two years later. His administration represented the culmination at the national level of the progressive movement that had been gathering strength since the turn of the century. His record in foreign policy was more mixed—and he saw his most cherished dream, American adherence to the League of Nations, blasted. Yet his legacy, for good or ill, continues to exert a powerful influence upon the world.

Wilson was not an easily approachable man at the personal level. Only to a few intimates could he unburden himself and express freely his innermost thoughts and feelings. His forte was in appealing to the minds and hearts of men in the mass. The excerpts in Part One from his writings, letters, and speeches are designed to illustrate the development of his career and ideas.

1
Scholar, Teacher, and University President

AT JOHNS HOPKINS

Attracted from boyhood by public affairs, Wilson had looked upon the law as a stepping-stone to a political career. But disillusioned by his experiences at the bar, he entered upon graduate study at Johns Hopkins University in the autumn of 1883. In this letter of October 30, 1883, to his fiancée, Ellen Louise Axson, he explains his decision.[1]

. . . I think that it is only very recently that I have known myself—indeed I am not altogether certain that the acquaintance is complete yet. Like everybody else I have learned chiefly by means of big mistakes. I've had to earn my own experience. It took me all my college days to learn that it was necessary and profitable to study. Having made that tardy discovery, I left college on the wrong tack. I had then, as I have still, a very earnest political creed and very pronounced political ambitions. I remember forming with Charlie Talcott (a class-mate and very intimate friend of mine) a solemn covenant that we would school all our powers and passions for the work of establishing the principles we held in common; that we would acquire knowledge that we might have power; and that we would drill ourselves in all the arts of persuasion, but especially in oratory (for he was a born orator if any man ever was), that we might have facility in leading others into our ways of thinking and enlisting them in our purposes. And we didn't do this in merely boyish enthusiasm, though we were

---

[1] Arthur S. Link *et al.*, eds., *The Papers of Woodrow Wilson* (Princeton: Princeton University Press, 1966—), II, 499–502. Volume II copyright © 1967 by Princeton University Press. Reprinted by permission of Princeton University Press.

blinded by a very boyish assurance with regard to the future and
our ability to mould the world as our hands might please. It was
not so long ago but that I can still feel the glow and the pulsations
of the hopes and the purposes of that moment—nay, it was not so
long ago but that I still retain some of the faith that then prompted
me. But a man has to know the world before he can work in it
to any purpose. He has to know the forces with which he must
coöperate and those with which he must contend; must know how
and where he can make himself felt, not reckoning according to the
conditions and possibilities of past times but according to a full
knowledge of the conditions of the present and the possibilities of
the immediate future. He must know the times into which he has
been born: and this I did *not* know when I left college and chose
my profession, as I proved by my choice. The profession I chose
was politics; the profession I entered was the law. I entered the one
because I thought it would lead to the other. It was once the sure
road; and Congress is still full of lawyers. But this is the time of
leisured classes—or, at least, that time is very near at hand—and
the time of crowded professions. It is plain to see why lawyers used
to be the only politicians. In a new country, in communities where
every man had his bread to earn, they were the only men (except
the minister and the physician) who stopped amidst the general
hurry of life to get learning; and they were the only men, without
exception, who were skilled in those arts of forensic contest that
were calculated to fit men for entering the lists at political tilts, or
for holding their own in legislative debate. They could hope, too,
when a turn of parties might have come, or their own popularity
might have waned, to return to their places at the bar to find a
place still open for them, to find themselves not altogether and
hopelessly crowded out; they could even, like Webster and Jeremiah
Mason and many others of less genius, make law and statecraft live
and thrive together, pleading causes in the courts even while holding seats in the Senate or leading parties in the House.

But those times are passing away. A man who has to earn a livelihood cannot nowadays turn aside from his trade for intervals of
officeholding and political activity. He cannot even do two things
at once. He is constrained by a minute division of labour to bend
all his energies to the one thing that is nearest at hand. Even in the

law men are becoming specialists. The whole field of legal knowledge, which former generations of American lawyers have superficially worked, is too big for any one man now, and practitioners are contenting themselves with cultivating small corners of it, digging deep and getting large crops out of small areas. And of course these small tenant farmers have to work much more diligently than did the great proprietors of former times. The law is more than ever before a jealous mistress. Whoever thinks, as I thought, that he can practice law successfully and study history and politics at the same time is wofully [sic] mistaken. If he is to make a living at the bar he must be a lawyer *and nothing else*. Of course he can compass a certain sort of double-calling success by dint of dishonesty. He can obtain, and betray, clients by pretending a knowledge of the law which he does not possess; and he can often gain political office by the arts of the demagogue. But he cannot be both a learned lawyer and a profound and public-spirited statesman, if he must plunge into practice and make the law a means of support.

In a word, my ambition could not be fulfilled at the bar; the studies for which I was best fitted, both by nature and by acquired habit, were not legitimate in a law office, and I was compelled in very justice to myself to seek some profession in which they would be legitimate. Evidently, however there was small latitude of choice. A professorship was the only feasible place for me, the only place that would afford leisure for reading and for original work, the only strictly literary berth with an income attached. True, professorships were scarce and hard to get, and professors could not participate actively in public affairs; but even a professorship might be gotten as soon as a competence at the bar, and the occupancy of office had never been an essential part of my political programme. Indeed I knew very well that a man without independent fortune must in any event content himself with becoming an *outside* force in politics, and I was well enough satisfied with the prospect of having whatever influence I might be able to exercise make itself felt through literary and non-partisan agencies: for my predilections, ever since I had any that were definite, have always turned very strongly towards a literary life, notwithstanding my decided taste for oratory, which is supposed to be the peculiar province of public men. . . .

STUDENT OF AMERICAN POLITICAL INSTITUTIONS

Wilson's most important contribution to scholarship was his classic study, Congressional Government, *written as his doctoral dissertation at Johns Hopkins, in which he shows his astute understanding of how Congress works, expresses his unhappiness over the expansion of congressional power vis-à-vis the executive, and reveals his admiration for the British system of responsible parliamentary government.*[2]

. . . It might reasonably have been expected that the prerogatives of the President would have been one of the most effectual restraints upon the power of Congress. He was constituted one of the three great coördinate branches of the government; his functions were made of the highest dignity; his privileges many and substantial—so great, indeed, that it has pleased the fancy of some writers to parade them as exceeding those of the British crown; and there can be little doubt that, had the presidential chair always been filled by men of commanding character, of acknowledged ability, and of thorough political training, it would have continued to be a seat of the highest authority and consideration, the true centre of the federal structure, the real throne of administration, and the frequent source of policies. . . . But the prestige of the presidential office has declined with the character of the Presidents. And the character of the Presidents has declined as the perfection of selfish party tactics has advanced.

It was inevitable that it should be so. After independence of choice on the part of the presidential electors had given place to the choice of presidential candidates by party conventions, it became absolutely necessary, in the eyes of politicians, and more and more necessary as time went on, to make expediency and availability the only rules of selection. As each party, when in convention assembled, spoke only those opinions which seemed to have received the sanction of the general voice, carefully suppressing in its "platform" all unpopular political tenets, and scrupulously omit-

[2] Woodrow Wilson, *Congressional Government: A Study in American Politics* (Boston: Houghton, Mifflin, 1885), pp. 41–45, 67, 69–70, 78–79, 92–95, 97–99.

ting mention of every doctrine that might be looked upon as characteristic and as part of a peculiar and original programme, so, when the presidential candidate came to be chosen, it was recognized as imperatively necessary that he should have as short a political record as possible, and that he should wear a clean and irreproachable insignificance. . . .

I am disposed to think, however, that the decline in the character of the Presidents is not the cause, but only the accompanying manifestation, of the declining prestige of the presidential office. That high office has fallen from its first estate of dignity because its power has waned; and its power has waned because the power of Congress has become predominant. . . .

. . . Congress was very quick and apt in learning what it could do and in getting into thoroughly good trim to do it. It very early divided itself into standing committees which it equipped with very comprehensive and thorough-going privileges of legislative initiative and control, and set itself through these to administer the government. . . . Accordingly it has entered more and more into the details of administration, until it has virtually taken into its own hands all the substantial powers of government. . . .

. . . Both the House of Representatives and the Senate conduct their business by what may figuratively, but not inaccurately, be called an odd device of *disintegration*. The House virtually both deliberates and legislates in small sections. Time would fail it to discuss all the bills brought in, for they every session number thousands; and it is to be doubted whether, even if time allowed, the ordinary processes of debate and amendment would suffice to sift the chaff from the wheat in the bushels of bills every week piled upon the clerk's desk. Accordingly, no futile attempt is made to do anything of the kind. The work is parceled out, most of it to the forty-seven Standing Committees which constitute the regular organization of the House, some of it to select committees appointed for special and temporary purposes. . . .

Of course it goes without saying that the practical effect of this Committee organization of the House is to consign to each of the Standing Committees the entire direction of legislation upon those subjects which properly come to its considerations. . . .

. . . In form, the Committees only digest the various matter introduced by individual members, and prepare it, with care, and after thorough investigation, for the final consideration and action of the House; but, in reality, they dictate the course to be taken, prescribing the decisions of the House not only, but measuring out, according to their own wills, its opportunities for debate and deliberation as well. The House sits, not for serious discussion, but to sanction the conclusions of its Committees as rapidly as possible. It legislates in its committee-rooms; not by the determinations of majorities, but by the resolutions of specially-commissioned minorities; so that it is not far from the truth to say that Congress in session is Congress on public exhibition, whilst Congress in its committee-rooms is Congress at work. . . .

. . . [As a result, power] is nowhere concentrated; it is rather deliberately and of set policy scattered amongst many small chiefs. It is divided up, as it were, into forty-seven seigniories, in each of which a Standing Committee is the court-baron and its chairman lord-proprietor. These petty barons, some of them not a little powerful, but none of them within reach of the full powers of rule, may at will exercise an almost despotic sway within their own shires, and may sometimes threaten to convulse even the realm itself; but both their mutual jealousies and their brief and restricted opportunities forbid their combining, and each is very far from the office of common leader.

I know that to some this scheme of distributed power and disintegrated rule seems a very excellent device whereby we are enabled to escape a dangerous "one-man power" and an untoward concentration of functions. . . .

It seems evident, however, when the question is looked at from another stand-point, that, as a matter of fact and experience, the more power is divided the more irresponsible it becomes. A mighty baron who can call half the country to arms is watched with greater jealousy, and, therefore, restrained with more vigilant care than is ever vouchsafed the feeble master of a single and solitary castle. . . .

. . . In the British House of Commons the functions and privileges of our Standing Committees are all concentrated in the hands of the Ministry, who have, besides, some prerogatives of leadership which even our Committees do not possess, so that they carry all responsibility as well as great power, and all debate wears an intense personal and party interest. Every important discussion is an arraignment of the Ministry by the Opposition—an arraignment of the majority by the minority; and every important vote is a party defeat and a party triumph. . . .

. . . Looking at government from a practical and business-like, rather than from a theoretical and abstractly-ethical point of view —treating the business of government as a business—it seems to be unquestionably and in a high degree desirable that all legislation should represent the action of parties as parties. . . . It should be desired that parties should act in distinct organizations, in accordance with avowed principles, under easily recognized leaders, in order that the voters might be able to declare by their ballots, not only their condemnation of any past policy, by withdrawing all support from the party responsible for it; but also and particularly their will as to the future administration of the government, by bringing into power a party pledged to the adoption of an acceptable policy.

It is, therefore, a fact of the most serious consequence that by our system of congressional rule no such means of controlling legislation is afforded. Outside of Congress the organization of the national parties is exceedingly well-defined and tangible; no one could wish it, and few could imagine it, more so; but within Congress it is obscure and intangible. Our parties marshal their adherents with the strictest possible discipline for the purpose of carrying elections, but their discipline is very slack and indefinite in dealing with legislation. At least there is within Congress no *visible*, and therefore no *controllable* party organization. The only bond of cohesion is the caucus, which occasionally whips a party together for coöperative action against the time for casting its vote upon some critical question. There is always a majority and a minority, indeed, but the legislation of a session does not represent the policy of either; it is simply an aggregate of the bills recommended by Committees composed of members from both sides of the House, and it is known to be usually, not the work of the majority men upon the Committees, but compromise conclusions bearing some shade or tinge of each of the variously-colored opinions and wishes of the committee-men of both parties.

It is plainly the representation of both parties on the Committees that makes party responsibility indistinct and organized party action almost impossible. If the Committees were composed entirely of members of the majority, and were thus constituted

representatives of the party in power, the whole course of congressional proceedings would unquestionably take on a very different aspect. There would then certainly be a compact opposition to
face the organized majority. . . .

EDUCATIONAL REFORMER

> *Wilson's struggle at Princeton, first over the eating clubs,
> then over the role and location of the graduate school, grew
> out of his interest in improving the quality of undergraduate
> education. In his 1909 essay "What Is a College For?" Wilson
> explains his larger purpose.*[3]

. . . What has happened is, in general terms, this: that the
work of the college, the work of its classrooms and laboratories, has
become the merely formal and compulsory side of its life, and that
a score of other things, lumped under the term "undergraduate activities," have become the vital, spontaneous, absorbing realities for
nine out of every ten men who go to college. These activities em-
brace social, athletic, dramatic, musical, literary, religious, and
professional organizations of every kind, besides many organized
for mere amusement and some, of great use and dignity, which
seek to exercise a general oversight and sensible direction of college
ways and customs. Those which consume the most time are, of
course, the athletic, dramatic, and musical clubs, whose practices,
rehearsals, games, and performances fill the term time and the brief
vacations alike. But it is the social organizations into which the
thought, the energy, the initiative, the enthusiasm of the largest
number of men go, and go in lavish measure.

The chief of these social organizations are residential families—
fraternities, clubs, groups of house-mates of one kind or another—
in which, naturally enough, all the undergraduate interests, all the
undergraduate activities of the college have their vital centre. . . .

. . . The college having determined, wisely enough, some generation or two ago, not to be any longer a boarding-school, has resolved itself into a mere teaching machine, with the necessary lec-

[3] Woodrow Wilson, "What Is a College For?" *Scribner's Magazine*, XLVI,
No. 5 (November, 1909), 574–77.

ture rooms and laboratories attached, . . . and has resigned into the hands of the undergraduates themselves the whole management of their life outside the classroom; and not only its management but also the setting up of all its machinery of every kind—as much as they please—and the constitution of its whole environment, so that teachers and pupils are not members of one university body but constitute two bodies sharply distinguished—and the undergraduate body the more highly organized and independent of the two. They parley with one another, but they do not live with one another, and it is much easier for the influence of the highly organized and very self-conscious undergraduate body to penetrate the faculty than it is for the influence of the faculty to permeate the undergraduates. . . .

. . . The consequences have been very important and very far-reaching. It is easy now to see that if you leave undergraduates entirely to themselves, to organize their own lives while in college as they please—and organize it in some way they must if thus cast adrift—that life, and not the deeper interests of the university, will presently dominate their thoughts, their imaginations, their favourite purposes. And not only that. The work of administering this complex life, with all its organizations and independent interests, successfully absorbs the energies, the initiative, the planning and originating powers of the best men among the undergraduates. . . . The very men the teacher most desires to get hold of and to enlist in some enterprise of the mind, the very men it would most reward him to instruct and whose training would count for most in leadership outside of college, in the country at large, and for the promotion of every interest the nation has, the natural leaders and doers, are drawn off and monopolized by these necessary and engaging undergraduate undertakings. The born leaders and managers and originators are drafted off to "run the college" (it is in fact nothing less), and the classroom, the laboratory, the studious conference with instructors get only the residuum of their attention, only what can be spared of their energy—are secondary matters where they ought to come first. It is the organization that is at fault, not the persons who enter into it and are moulded by it. It cannot turn out otherwise in the circumstances. The side shows are so numerous, so diverting—so important, if you will—that they have swallowed up the circus, and those who perform in the main tent must often whistle for their audiences, discouraged and humiliated.

Such is college life nowadays, and such its relation to college work and the all-important intellectual interests which the colleges are endowed and maintained to foster. I need not stop to argue that the main purposes of education cannot be successfully realized under such conditions. I need not stop to urge that the college was not and can never be intended for the uses it is now being put to. . . . Amusement, athletic games, the zest of contest and competition, the challenge there is in most college activities to the instinct of initiative and the gifts of leadership and achievement—all these are wholesome means of stimulation, which keep young men from going stale and turning to things that demoralize. But they should not assume the front of the stage where more serious and lasting interests are to be served. Men cannot be prepared by them for modern life.

The college is meant for a severer, more definite discipline than this: a discipline which will fit men for the contests and achievements of an age whose every task is conditioned upon some intelligent and effective use of the mind, upon some substantial knowledge, some special insight, some trained capacity, some penetration which comes from study, not from natural readiness or mere practical experience.

The side shows need not be abolished. They need not be cast out or even discredited. But they must be subordinated. They must be put in their natural place as diversions, and ousted from their present dignity and preëminence as occupations. . . .

. . . [A] new discipline is desirable, is absolutely necessary, if the college is to be recalled to its proper purpose, its bounden duty. It cannot perform its duty as it is now organized.

The fundamental thing to be accomplished in the new organization is, that, instead of being the heterogeneous congeries of petty organizations it now is, instead of being allowed to go to pieces in a score of fractions free to cast off from the whole as they please, it should be drawn together again into a single university family of which the teachers shall be as natural and as intimate members as the undergraduates. The "life" of the college should not be separated from its chief purposes and most essential objects, should not be contrasted with its duties and in rivalry with them.

The two should be but two sides of one and the same thing; the association of men, young and old, for serious mental endeavour and also, in the intervals of work, for every wholesome sport and diversion. Undergraduate life should not be in rivalry and contrast with undergraduate duties: undergraduates should not be merely in attendance upon the college, but parts of it on every side of its life, very conscious and active parts. They should consciously live its whole life—not under masters, as in school, and yet associated in some intimate daily fashion with their masters in learning: so that learning may not seem one thing and life another. The organizations whose objects lie outside study should be but parts of the whole, not set against it, but included within it.

All this can be accomplished by a comparatively simple change of organization which will make master and pupil members of the same free, self-governed family, upon natural terms of intimacy. . . .

But as the struggle grew increasingly bitter, Wilson came more and more—as his remarks before a gathering of Princeton alumni at Pittsburgh, April 16, 1910, reveal—to view the issue as a conflict of democracy versus special privilege.[4]

How does the nation judge Princeton? The institution is intended for the service of the country, and it is by the requirements of the country that it will be measured. I trust I may be thought among the last to blame the churches, yet I feel it my duty to say that they—at least the Protestant churches—are serving the classes and not the masses of the people. They have more regard for the pew rents than for men's souls. They are depressing the level of Christian endeavor.

It is the same with the universities. We look for the support of the wealthy and neglect our opportunities to serve the people. It is for this reason the State University is held in popular approval while the privately supported institution to which we belong is coming to suffer a corresponding loss of esteem.

While attending a recent Lincoln celebration I asked myself if Lincoln would have been as serviceable to the people of this coun-

[4] Ray Stannard Baker and William E. Dodd, eds., *The Public Papers of Woodrow Wilson* (New York: Harper & Brothers, 1925–27), II, 202–3.

try had he been a college man, and I was obliged to say to myself that he would not. The process to which the college man is subjected does not render him serviceable to the country as a whole. It is for this reason that I have dedicated every power in me to a democratic regeneration.

The American college must become saturated in the same sympathies as the common people. The colleges of this country must be reconstructed from the top to the bottom. The American people will tolerate nothing that savours of exclusiveness. Their political parties are going to pieces. They are busy with their moral regeneration and they want leaders who can help them accomplish it. Only those leaders who seem able to promise something of a moral advance are able to secure a following. The people are tired of pretense, and I ask you, as Princeton men, to heed what is going on. . . .

2

The Road to the White House

THE POLITICAL CONSERVATIVE

While never a dogmatic apostle of laissez-faire, Wilson re-
mained while president of Princeton basically a states' rights
Jeffersonian who looked with deep suspicion upon proposals
for government—above all, federal government—regulation of
business. Although conceding that evils had emerged within
the system, he urged reliance upon the courts to punish busi-
ness wrongdoing.[1]

. . . There is a great and apparently growing body of opinion
in the country which approves of a radical change in the character
of our institutions and the objects of our law, which wishes to see
government, and the federal government at that, regulate business.
Some men who entertain this wish perceive that it is socialistic,
some do not. But of course it is socialistic. Government cannot
properly or intelligently regulate business without fully compre-
hending it in its details as well as in its larger aspects; it cannot
comprehend it except through the instrumentality of expert commissions; it cannot use expert commissions long for purposes of
regulation without itself by degrees undertaking actually to order
and conduct what it began by regulating. We are at present on
the high road to government ownership of many sorts, or to some
other method of control which will in practice be as complete as
actual ownership.

On the other hand, there is a great body of opinion, slow to
express itself, sorely perplexed in the presence of modern business
conditions, but very powerful and upon the eve of an uprising,
which prefers the older and simpler methods of the law, prefers

---

[1] Woodrow Wilson, "Politics (1857–1907)," *Atlantic Monthly*, Vol. C, No. 5
(November, 1907), 645–46.

courts to commissions, and believes them, if properly used and adapted, better, more efficacious, in the end more purifying, than the new instrumentalities now being so unthinkingly elaborated. The country is still full of men who retain a deep enthusiasm for the old ideals of individual liberty, sobered and kept within bounds by the equally old definitions of personal responsibility, the ancient safeguards against license; and these men are right in believing that those older principles can be so used as to control modern business and keep government outside the pale of industrial enterprise. The law can deal with transactions instead of with methods of business, and with individuals instead of with corporations. It can reverse the process which creates corporations, and instead of compounding individuals, oblige corporations to analyze their organization and name the individuals responsible for each class of their transactions. The law, both civil and criminal, can clearly enough characterize transactions, can clearly enough determine what their consequences shall be to the individuals who engage in them in a responsible capacity. New definitions in that field are not beyond the knowledge of modern lawyers or the skill of modern lawmakers, if they will accept the advice of disinterested lawyers. We shall never moralize society by fining or even dissolving corporations; we shall only inconvenience it. We shall moralize it only when we make up our minds as to what transactions are reprehensible, and bring those transactions home to individuals with the full penalties of the law. That is the other, the greater body of opinion; one or other of the great parties of the nation must sooner or later stand with it, while the other stands with those who burden government with the regulation of business by direct oversight. . . .

> *In line with his deep-seated conservatism, Wilson in the years before his election to the governorship of New Jersey belonged to the Grover Cleveland–sound money wing of the Democratic party. And in his frank comment to Princeton trustee Adrian Joline, April 29, 1907, he makes no bones about his distaste for William Jennings Bryan.*[2]

[2] Quoted in Ray Stannard Baker, *Woodrow Wilson: Life and Letters* (Garden City, N.Y.: Doubleday, Page & Company, 1927–39), III, 23. All quotations from this volume are reprinted by permission of Mrs. Rachel Baker Napier in behalf of the heirs of Ray Stannard Baker.

Would that we could do something, at once, dignified and effective, to knock Mr. Bryan, once for all, into a cocked hat.

MOVING TOWARD PROGRESSIVISM

By the end of his campaign for governor of New Jersey, however, Wilson had emerged as the champion of many of the reform goals of the day. This shift came about partly because of his unhappy experiences at Princeton, partly because of political expediency, and partly because his campaigning forced him to rethink his premises and principles. In his inaugural address as governor, he sets forth his new-found reform program.[3]

. . . The whole world has changed within the lifetime of men not yet in their thirties; the world of business, and therefore the world of society and the world of politics. The organization and movement of business are new and upon a novel scale. Business has changed so rapidly that for a long time we were confused, alarmed, bewildered, in a sort of terror of the things we had ourselves raised up. We talked about them either in sensational articles in the magazines which distorted every line of the picture, or in conservative editorials in our newspapers, which stoutly denied that anything at all had happened, or in grave discourses which tried to treat them as perfectly normal phenomena, or in legislative debates which sought to govern them with statutes which matched them neither in size nor in shape.

But, if only by sheer dint of talking about them, either to frighten or to reassure one another, or to make ourselves out wiser or more knowing than our fellows, we have at last turned them about and looked at them from almost every angle and begin to see them whole, as they are. Corporations are no longer hobgoblins which have sprung at us out of some mysterious ambush, nor yet unholy inventions of rascally rich men, nor yet the puzzling devices by which ingenious lawyers build up huge rights out of a multitude of small wrongs; but merely organizations of a perfectly intelligible

[3] Ray Stannard Baker and William E. Dodd, eds., *The Public Papers of Woodrow Wilson* (New York: Harper & Brothers, 1925–27), II, 270–79, 281–82.

sort which the law has licensed for the convenience of extensive business; organizations which have proved very useful but which have for the time being slipped out of the control of the very law that gave them leave to be and that can make or unmake them at pleasure. We have now to set ourselves to control them, soberly but effectively, and to bring them thoroughly within the regulation of the law.

There is a great opportunity here; for wise regulation, wise adjustment, will mean the removal of half the difficulties that now beset us in our search for justice and equality and fair chances of fortune for the individuals who make up our modern society. And there is a great obligation as well as a great opportunity, an imperative obligation, from which we cannot escape if we would. Public opinion is at last wide awake. It begins to understand the problems to be dealt with; it begins to see very clearly indeed the objects to be sought. It knows what has been going on. It sees where resistance has come from whenever efforts at reform have been made, and knows also the means of resistance that have been resorted to. It is watchful, insistent, suspicious. No man who wishes to enjoy the public confidence dare hold back, and, if he is wise, he will not resort to subterfuge. A duty is exacted of him which he must perform simply, directly, immediately. The gate of opportunity stands wide open. If we are foolish enough to be unwilling to pass through it, the whip of opinion will drive us through.

No wise man will say, of course, that he sees the whole problem of reform lying plain before him, or knows how to frame the entire body of law that will be necessary to square business with the general interest, and put right and fairness and public spirit in the saddle again in all the transactions of our new society; but some things are plain enough, and upon these we can act.

In the first place, it is plain that our laws with regard to the relations of employer and employe are in many respects wholly antiquated and impossible. They were framed for another age, which nobody now living remembers, which is, indeed, so remote from our life that it would be difficult for many of us to understand it if it were described to us. The employer is now generally a corporation or huge company of some kind; the employe is one of hundreds or of thousands brought together, not by individual masters whom they know and with whom they have personal relations, but by agents of one sort or another. Workingmen are marshalled in great numbers for the performance of a multitude of particular tasks under a common discipline. They generally use dangerous and powerful machinery, over whose repair and renewal they have no control. New rules must be devised with regard to their obligations and their rights, their obligations to their employers and their responsibilities to one another. New rules must be devised for their protection, for their compensation when injured, for their support when disabled. . . .

. . . We must have a workingman's compensation act, which will not put upon [the individual workingman] the burden of fighting powerful composite employers to obtain his rights, but which will give him his rights without suit, directly, and without contest, by automatic operation of law, as if of a law of insurance.

This is the first adjustment needed, because it affects the rights, the happiness, the lives and fortunes of the largest number, and because it is the adjustment for which justice cries loudest and with the most direct appeal to our hearts as well as to our consciences.

But there is regulation needed which lies back of that and is much more fundamental. The composite employer himself needs to have his character and powers overhauled, his constitution and rights reconsidered, readjusted to the fundamental and abiding interests of society. If I may speak very plainly, we are much too free with grants of charters to corporations in New Jersey: A corporation exists, not of natural right, but only by license of law, and the law, if we look at the matter in good conscience, is responsible for what it creates. It can never rightly authorize any kind of fraud or imposition. It cannot righteously allow the setting up of a business which has no sound basis, or which follows methods which in any way outrage justice or fair dealing or the principles of honest industry. The law cannot give its license to things of that kind. It thereby authenticates what it ought of right to forbid.

I would urge, therefore, the imperative obligation of public policy and of public honesty we are under to effect such changes in the law of the State as will henceforth effectually prevent the abuse of the privilege of incorporation which has in recent years brought so much discredit upon our State. In order to do this it will be necessary to regulate and restrict the issue of securities, to enforce regulations with regard to bona fide capital, examining very rigorously the basis of capitalization, and to prescribe methods by which the public shall be safeguarded against fraud, deception, extortion, and every abuse of its confidence.

And such scrutiny and regulation ought not to be confined to corporations seeking charters. They ought also to be extended to corporations already operating under the license and authority of the State. For the right to undertake such regulation is susceptible of easy and obvious justification. . . . These modern enterprises . . . conduct business transactions whose scope and influence are as wide as whole regions of the Union, often as wide as the nation itself. They affect sometimes the lives and fortunes of whole communities, dominate prices, determine land values, make and unmake markets, develop or check the growth of city and of countryside. If law is at liberty to adjust the general conditions of society itself, it is at liberty to control these great instrumentalities which nowadays, in so large part, determine the character of society. Wherever we can find what the common interest is in respect of them we shall find a solid enough basis for law, for reform.

The matter is most obvious when we turn to what we have come to designate public service, or public utility, corporations—those which supply us with the means of transportation and with those common necessaries, water, light, heat, and power. Here are corporations exercising peculiar and extraordinary franchises, and bearing such a relation to society in respect of the services they render that it may be said that they are the very medium of its life. They render a public and common service of which it is necessary that practically everybody should avail himself.

We have a Public Utilities Commission in New Jersey, but it has hardly more than powers of inquiry and advice. It could even as it stands be made a powerful instrument of publicity and of opinion, but it may also modestly wait until it is asked before expressing a judgment, and in any case it will have the uncomfortable consciousness that its opinion is gratuitous, and carries no weight of effective authority. This will not do. It is understood by everybody who knows anything of the common interest that it must have complete regulative powers: the power to regulate rates, the power to learn and make public everything that should furnish a basis for the public judgment with regard to the soundness, the efficiency, the economy of the business—the power, in brief, to adjust such service at every point and in every respect, whether of equipment or charges or methods of financing or means of service, to the general interest of the communities affected. This can be done, as experience elsewhere has demonstrated, not only without destroying the profits of such business, but also with the effect of putting it upon a more satisfactory footing for those who conduct it no less than for those who make use of it day by day.

Such regulation, based on thorough and authoritative inquiry, will go far towards disclosing and establishing those debatable values upon which so many questions of taxation turn. There is an uneasy feeling throughout the State, in which, I dare say, we all share, that there are glaring inequalities in our system—or, at any rate, in our practice—of taxation. The most general complaint is, that there is great inequality as between individuals and corporations. I do not see how anyone can determine whether there are or not, for we have absolutely no uniform system of assessment. It would seem that in every locality there is some local variety of practice, in the rate, the ratio of assessment value to market value, and that every assessor is a law unto himself. Our whole system of taxation, which is no system at all, needs overhauling from top to bottom. There can be no system, no safety, no regulation in a multitude of boards. An efficient Public Utilities Commission will be a beginning towards a system of taxation as well as towards a system of corporate control. We cannot fairly tax values until we have ascertained and established them.

And the great matter of conservation seems to me like a part of the same subject. The safeguarding of our water supply, the purification of our streams in order to maintain them as sources of life, and their protection against those who would divert them or diminish their volume for private profit, the maintenance of such woodlands as are left us and the reforestation of bare tracts more suited for forest than for field, the sanitation of great urban districts such as cover the northern portions of our State, by thorough systems of drainage and of refuse disposal, the protection of the public health and the facilitation of urban and suburban life—these are all public obligations which fall sooner or later upon you as the lawmakers of the commonwealth, and they are all parts of the one great task of adjustment which has fallen to our generation. Our business is to adjust right to right, interest to interest, and to systematize right and convenience, individual rights and corporate privileges, upon the single basis of the general good, the good of whole communities, the good which no one will look after or suffice to secure if the legislator does not, the common good for whose safeguarding and maintenance government is intended.

This readjustment has not been going on very fast or very favorably in New Jersey. It has been observed that it limped, or was prevented, or neglected, in other States as well. Everywhere there has been confusion of counsel and many a sad miscarriage of plan. There have, consequently, been some very radical criticisms of our methods of political action. There is widespread dissatisfaction with what our legislatures do, and still more serious dissatisfaction with what they do not do. Some persons have said that representative government has proved too indirect and clumsy an instrument, and has broken down as a means of popular control. Others, looking a little deeper, have said that it was not representative government that had broken down, but the effort to get it. They have pointed out that with our present methods of machine nomination and our present methods of elections, which were nothing more than a choice between one set of machine nominees and another, we did not get representative government at all—at least not government representative of the people, but government representative of political managers who served their own interests and the interests of those with whom they found it profitable to establish partnerships.

Obviously this is something that goes to the root of the whole matter. Back of all reform lies the method of getting it. Back of the question what you want lies the question, the fundamental question of all government, how are you going to get it? How are you going to get public servants who will obtain it for you? How are you going to get genuine representatives who will serve your real interests, and not their own or the interests of some special group or body of your fellow-citizens whose power is of the few and not of the many? These are the queries which have drawn the attention of the whole country to the subject of the direct primary, the direct choice of representatives by the people, without the intervention of the nominating machine, the nominating organization.

I earnestly commend to your careful consideration in this connection the laws in recent years adopted in the State of Oregon, whose effect has been to bring government back to the people and to protect it from the control of the representatives of selfish and special interests. They seem to me to point the direction which we must also take before we have completed our regeneration of a government which has suffered so seriously and so long as ours has here in New Jersey from private management and organized selfishness. Our primary laws, extended and perfected, will pave the way. They should be extended to every elective office, and to the selection of every party committee or official as well, in order that the people may once for all take charge of their own affairs, their own political organization and association, and the methods of primary selection should be so perfected that the primaries will be put upon the same free footing that the methods of election themselves are meant to rest upon.

We have here the undoubtedly sound chain and sequency of reforms: an actual direct choice by the people of the men who are to organize alike their parties and their government, and those measures which true representatives of the people will certainly favour and adopt—systematic compensation for injured workingmen; the careful regulation in the common interest of all corporations, both in respect of their organization and of their methods of business, and especially of public service corporations; the equalization of taxes; and the conservation of the natural resources of the State and of the health and safety of its people.

Another matter of the most vital consequence goes with all these: namely, systematic ballot reform and thorough and stringent provisions of law against corrupt practices in connection alike with primaries and with elections. We have lagged behind our sister States in these important matters, and should make haste to avail ourselves of their example and their experience. Here, again, Oregon may be our guide.

This is a big programme, but it is a perfectly consistent programme, and a perfectly feasible programme, and one upon whose details it ought to be possible to agree even within the limits of a single legislative session. You may count upon my coöperation at every step of the work. . . .

We are servants of the people, of the whole people. Their interest should be our constant study. We should pursue it without fear or favour. Our reward will be greater than that to be obtained in any other service: the satisfaction of furthering large ends, large purposes, of being an intimate part of that slow but constant and ever hopeful force of liberty and of enlightenment that is lifting mankind from age to age to new levels of progress and achievement, and of having been something greater than successful men. For we shall have been instruments of humanity, men whose thought was not for themselves, but for the true and lasting comfort and happiness of men everywhere. It is not the foolish ardour of too sanguine or too radical reform that I urge upon you, but merely the tasks that are evident and pressing, the things we have knowledge and guidance enough to do; and to do with confidence and energy. I merely point out the present business of progressive and serviceable government, the next stage on the journey of duty. The path is as inviting as it is plain. Shall we hesitate to tread it? I look forward with genuine pleasure to the prospect of being your comrade upon it.

GOVERNOR OF NEW JERSEY

As governor, Wilson first established his credentials as a progressive by defeating the senatorial bid of Democratic party boss James S. Smith, Jr., and then went on to push through the legislature a far-reaching program of reform that brought him national attention. In this letter to Mrs. Mary A. Hulbert, April 23, 1911, he describes his achievements.[4]

The Legislature adjourned yesterday morning at three o'clock, with its work done. I got absolutely everything I strove for—and more besides: all four of the great acts that I had set my heart on (the primaries and election law, the corrupt practices act, as stringent as the English, the workingmen's compensation act, and the act giving a public commission control over the railways, the trolley lines, the water companies, and the gas and electric light and power companies), and besides them I got certain fundamental school reforms and an act enabling any city in the State to adopt the commission form of government, which simplifies the electoral process and concentrates responsibility. Everyone, the papers included, are saying that none of it could have been done, if it had not been for

[4] Quoted in Baker, *Woodrow Wilson*, III, 169–71.

my influence and tact and hold upon the people. Be that as it may, the thing was done, and the result was as complete a victory as has ever been won, I venture to say, in the history of the country. I wrote the platform, I had the measures formulated to my mind, I kept the pressure of opinion constantly on the legislature, and the programme was carried out to its last detail. This with the senatorial business seems, in the minds of the people looking on little less than a miracle, in the light of what has been the history of reform hitherto in this State. As a matter of fact, it is just a bit of natural history. I came to the office in the fulness of time, when opinion was ripe on all these matters, when both parties were committed to these reforms, and by merely standing fast, and by never losing sight of the business for an hour, but keeping up all sorts of (legitimate) pressure *all the time,* kept the mighty forces from being diverted or blocked at any point. The strain has been immense, but the reward is great. I feel a great reaction to-day, for I am, of course, exceedingly tired, but I am quietly and deeply happy that I should have been of just the kind of service I wished to be to those who elected and trusted me. I can look them in the face, like a servant who has kept faith and done all that was in him, given every power he possessed, to them and their affairs. There could be no deeper source of satisfaction and contentment! I have no doubt that a good deal of the result was due to the personal relations I established with the men in the Senate, the Republican Senate which, it was feared at the outset, might be the stumbling block. You remember the dinner in New York and the supper at the Trenton country club which I described to you. Those evenings undoubtedly played their part in the outcome. They brought us all close together on terms not unlike friendly intimacy; made them realize just what sort of *person* I was. Since then Republicans have resorted to my office for counsel and advice almost as freely as Democrats (an almost unprecedented circumstance at Trenton) and with several of them I have established relations almost of affection. Otherwise I do not believe that the extraordinary thing that happened could possibly have come about: for all four of the great "administration" measures passed the Senate *without a dissenting voice!* . . .

. . . I have not felt that I could relax my attention for a moment while the session lasted—and it had already begun when I was inaugurated, you know, and plunged into the first fight, the fight for the senatorship. Winning that, by the way, made all the rest easier; but it also made the session some two weeks longer than usual. What a vigil it has been! I am certainly in training for almost anything that may come to me by way of public tasks. There are serious times ahead. It daunts me to think of the possibility of my playing an influential part in them. There is no telling what deep waters may be ahead of me. The forces of greed and the forces of justice and humanity are about to grapple for a bout in which men will spend all the life that is in them. God grant I may have strength enough to count, to tip the balance in the unequal and tremendous struggle! . . .

CAMPAIGNING FOR THE PRESIDENCY

In his 1912 campaign for the presidency, Wilson made the cornerstone of his program—which he called the New Freedom—his pledge to break the grip of monopolies upon the nation's business in order to open the doors of opportunity for the little man.[5]

Gentlemen say, they have been saying for a long time, and, therefore, I assume that they believe, that trusts are inevitable. They don't say that big business is inevitable. They don't say merely that the elaboration of business upon a great co-operative scale is characteristic of our time and has come about by the natural operation of modern civilization. We would admit that. But they say that the particular kind of combinations that are now controlling our economic development came into existence naturally and were inevitable; and that, therefore, we have to accept them as unavoidable and administer our development through them. . . .

I admit the popularity of the theory that the trusts have come about through the natural development of business conditions in

[5] Woodrow Wilson, *The New Freedom: A Call for the Emancipation of the Generous Energies of a People* (New York: Doubleday, Page & Company, 1913), pp. 163–70, 172–73, 177, 184–85, 190–91. Reprinted by permission of Dale D. Drain, Co-Executor of the Estate of Edith Bolling Wilson.

the United States, and that it is a mistake to try to oppose the processes by which they have been built up, because those processes belong to the very nature of business in our time, and that therefore the only thing we can do, and the only thing we ought to attempt to do, is to accept them as inevitable arrangements and make the best out of it that we can by regulation.

I answer, nevertheless, that this attitude rests upon a confusion of thought. Big business is no doubt to a large extent necessary and natural. The development of business upon a great scale, upon a great scale of co-operation, is inevitable, and, let me add, is probably desirable. But that is a very different matter from the development of trusts, because the trusts have not grown. They have been artificially created; they have been put together, not by natural processes, but by the will, the deliberate planning will, of men who were more powerful than their neighbors in the business world, and who wished to make their power secure against competition. . . .

Did you ever look into the way a trust was made? It is very natural, in one sense, in the same sense in which human greed is natural. If I haven't efficiency enough to beat my rivals, then the thing I am inclined to do is to get together with my rivals and say: "Don't let's cut each other's throats; let's combine and determine prices for ourselves; determine the output, and thereby determine the prices: and dominate and control the market." That is very natural. That has been done ever since freebooting was established. That has been done ever since power was used to establish control. The reason that the masters of combination have sought to shut out competition is that the basis of control under competition is brains and efficiency. I admit that any large corporation built up by the legitimate processes of business, by economy, by efficiency, is natural; and I am not afraid of it, no matter how big it grows. It can stay big only by doing its work more thoroughly than anybody else. And there is a point of bigness—as every business man in this country knows, though some of them will not admit it—where you pass the limit of efficiency and get into the region of clumsiness and unwieldiness. You can make your combine so extensive that you can't digest it into a single system; you can get so many parts that you can't assemble them as you would an effective piece of machinery. The point of efficiency is overstepped in the natural process of development oftentimes, and it has been overstepped many times in the artificial and deliberate formation of trusts. . . .

Talk of that as sound business? Talk of that as inevitable? It is based upon nothing except power. It is not based upon efficiency. It is no wonder that the big trusts are not prospering in proportion to such competitors as they still have in such parts of their business as competitors have access to. . . . Here we have a lot of giants staggering along under an almost intolerable weight of artificial burdens, which they have put on their own backs, and constantly looking about lest some little pigmy with a round stone in a sling may come out and slay them.

For my part, I want the pigmy to have a chance to come out. And I foresee a time when the pigmies will be so much more athletic, so much more astute, so much more active, than the giants, that it will be a case of Jack the giant-killer. Just let some of the youngsters I know have a chance and they'll give these gentlemen points. Lend them a little money. They can't get any now. See to it that when they have got a local market they can't be squeezed out of it. Give them a chance to capture that market and then see them capture another one and another one, until these men who are carrying an intolerable load of artificial securities find that they have got to get down to hard pan to keep their foothold at all. I am willing to let Jack come into the field with the giant, and if Jack has the brains that some Jacks that I know in America have, then I should like to see the giant get the better of him, with the load that he, the giant, has to carry—the load of water. For I'll undertake to put a water-logged giant out of business any time, if you will give me a fair field and as much credit as I am entitled to, and let the law do what from time immemorial law has been expected to do—see fair play. . . .

I take my stand absolutely, where every progressive ought to take his stand, on the proposition that private monopoly is indefensible and intolerable. And there I will fight my battle. And I know how to fight it. Everybody who has even read the newspapers knows the means by which these men built up their power and created these monopolies. Any decently equipped lawyer can suggest to you statutes by which the whole business can be stopped. What these gentlemen do not want is this: they do not want to be compelled to meet all comers on equal terms. I am perfectly willing that they should beat any competitor by fair means; but I know the foul means they have adopted, and I know that they can be stopped by law. If they think that coming into the market upon the basis of mere efficiency, upon the mere basis of knowing how to manufacture goods better than anybody else and to sell them cheaper than anybody else, they can carry the immense amount of water that they have put into their enterprises in order to buy up rivals, then they are perfectly welcome to try it. But there must be no squeezing out of the beginner, no crippling his credit; no discrimination against retailers who buy from a rival; no threats against concerns who sell supplies to a rival; no holding back of raw material from him; no secret arrangements against him. All the fair competition you choose, but no unfair competition of any kind. . . .

I have been told by a great many men that the idea I have, that by restoring competition you can restore industrial freedom, is based upon a failure to observe the actual happenings of the last decades in this country; because, they say, it is just free competition that has made it possible for the big to crush the little.

I reply, it is not free competition that has done that; it is illicit competition. It is competition of the kind that the law ought to stop, and can stop—this crushing of the little man. . . .

. . . There has come about an extraordinary and very sinister concentration in the control of business in the country. . . . It is more important still that the control of credit also has become dangerously centralized. It is the mere truth to say that the financial resources of the country are not at the command of those who do not submit to the direction and domination of small groups of capitalists who wish to keep the economic development of the country under their own eye and guidance. The great monopoly in this country is the monopoly of big credits. So long as that exists, our old variety and freedom and individual energy of development are out of the question. A great industrial nation is controlled by its system of credit. Our system of credit is privately concentrated. The growth of the nation, therefore, and all our activities are in the hands of a few men who, even if their action be honest and intended for the public interest, are necessarily concentrated upon the great undertakings in which their own money is involved and who necessarily, by very reason of their own limitations, chill and check and destroy genuine economic freedom. This is the greatest question of all, and to this statesmen must address themselves with an earnest determination to serve the long future and the true liberties of men. . . .

When we undertake the strategy which is going to be necessary to overcome and destroy this far-reaching system of monopoly, we are rescuing the business of this country, we are not injuring it. . . . Limit opportunity, restrict the field of originative achievement, and you have cut out the heart and root of all prosperity.

The only thing that can ever make a free country is to keep a free and hopeful heart under every jacket in it. Honest American industry has always thriven, when it has thriven at all, on freedom; it has never thriven on monopoly. It is a great deal better to shift for yourselves than to be taken care of by a great combination of capital. I, for my part, do not want to be taken care of. I would rather starve a free man than be fed a mere thing at the caprice of those who are organizing American industry as they please to organize it. I know, and every man in his heart knows, that the only way to enrich America is to make it possible for any man who has the brains to get into the game. I am not jealous of the size of any business that has grown to that size. I am not jealous of any process of growth, no matter how huge the result, provided the result was indeed obtained by the processes of wholesome development, which are the processes of efficiency, of economy, of intelligence, and of invention.

3

The Presidency

THE NEW FREEDOM

The first target of Wilson's New Freedom program was what he thought the most blatant form of special privilege— the protective tariff. Calling Congress into special session, he shattered precedent by appearing in person on April 8, 1913, to deliver his special message urging immediate downward revision of the Payne-Aldrich tariff.[1]

. . . I have called the Congress together in extraordinary session because a duty was laid upon the party now in power at the recent elections which it ought to perform promptly, in order that the burden carried by the people under existing law may be lightened as soon as possible, and in order, also, that the business interests of the country may not be kept too long in suspense as to what the fiscal changes are to be to which they will be required to adjust themselves. It is clear to the whole country that the tariff duties must be altered. They must be changed to meet the radical alteration in the conditions of our economic life which the country has witnessed within the last generation. While the whole face and method of our industrial and commercial life were being changed beyond recognition the tariff schedules have remained what they were before the change began, or have moved in the direction they were given when no large circumstance of our industrial development was what it is to-day. Our task is to square them with the actual facts. The sooner that is done the sooner we shall escape from suffering from the facts and the sooner our men of business will be free to thrive by the law of nature—the nature of free business—instead of by the law of legislation and artificial arrangement.

We have seen tariff legislation wander very far afield in our day—

[1] *Congressional Record,* 63rd Cong., 1st sess., L (1913), pt. 1, 130.

very far indeed from the field in which our prosperity might have had a normal growth and stimulation. No one who looks the facts squarely in the face or knows anything that lies beneath the surface of action can fail to perceive the principles upon which recent tariff legislation has been based. We long ago passed beyond the modest notion of "protecting" the industries of the country and moved boldly forward to the idea that they were entitled to the direct patronage of the Government. For a long time—a time so long that the men now active in public policy hardly remember the conditions that preceded it—we have sought in our tariff schedules to give each group of manufacturers or producers what they themselves thought that they needed in order to maintain a practically exclusive market as against the rest of the world. Consciously or unconsciously, we have built up a set of privileges and exemptions from competition behind which it was easy by any, even the crudest, forms of combination to organize monopoly; until at last nothing is normal, nothing is obliged to stand the tests of efficiency and economy, in our world of big business, but everything thrives by concerted arrangement. Only new principles of action will save us from a final hard crystallization of monopoly and a complete loss of the influences that quicken enterprise and keep independent energy alive.

It is plain what those principles must be. We must abolish everything that bears even the semblance of privilege or of any kind of artificial advantage, and put our business men and producers under the stimulation of a constant necessity to be efficient, economical, and enterprising, masters of competitive supremacy, better workers and merchants than any in the world. Aside from the duties laid upon articles which we do not, and probably can not, produce, therefore, and the duties laid upon luxuries and merely for the sake of the revenues they yield, the object of the tariff duties henceforth laid must be effective competition, the whetting of American wits by contest with the wits of the rest of the world. . . .

After his victory in the tariff fight, Wilson pushed on with the next two major items on his program—currency and banking reform and the trust problem. With the passage of the Federal Reserve Act (December, 1913) and the Federal Trade Commission and Clayton Antitrust acts (September and October, 1914), he regarded the New Freedom pro-

*gram as essentially completed. In the following public letter
of November 17, 1914, to Secretary of the Treasury William
A. McAdoo, upon the opening of the Federal Reserve banking
system, he explains how the reforms adopted will solve the
nation's major problems and indicates his belief that what the
country needs is a period of calm in which to adjust to the
new measures.*[2]

. . . We have only to look back ten years or so to realize the
deep perplexities and dangerous ill humors out of which we have
now at last issued as if from a bewildering fog, a noxious miasma.
Ten or twelve years ago the country was torn and excited by an agitation which shook the very foundations of her political life, brought
her business ideal into question, condemned her social standards,
denied the honesty of her men of affairs, the integrity of her economic processes, the morality and good faith of many of the things
which her law sustained.

Those who had power, whether in business or in politics, were
almost universally looked upon with suspicion, and little attempt
was made to distinguish the just from the unjust. They in their
turn seemed to distrust the people and to wish to limit their control.
There was ominous antagonism between classes. Capital and labor
were in sharp conflict without prospect of accommodation between
them. Interests harshly clashed which should have co-operated.

This was not merely the work of irresponsible agitators. There
were real wrongs which cried out to be righted and fearless men
had called attention to them, demanding that they be dealt with by
law. We were living under a tariff which had been purposely con-
trived to confer private favors upon those who were cooperating to
keep the party that originated it in power and in all that too fertile
soil all the bad, interlaced growth and jungle of monopoly had
sprung up. Credit, the very life of trade, the very air men must
breathe if they would meet their opportunities, was too largely in
control of the same small groups who had planted and cultivated
monopoly. The control of all big business, and, by consequence, of
all little business, too, was for the most part potentially, if not actu-

[2] Ray Stannard Baker and William E. Dodd, eds., *The Public Papers of
Woodrow Wilson* (New York: Harper & Brothers, 1925–27), III, 210–14.

ally, in their hands. And the thing stood so until the Democrats came into power last year. The legislation of the past year and a half has in very large measure done away with these things. With a correction, suspicion and ill-will will pass away. For not only have these things been righted, but new things have been put into action which are sure to prove the instruments of a new life, in which the mists and distempers which have so embarrassed us will be cleared away; the wrongs and misunderstandings corrected which have brought distrust upon so many honest men unjustly. That is the main ground of my own satisfaction.

The tariff has been recast with a view to supporting the Government rather than supporting the favored beneficiaries of the Government. A system of banking and currency issues has been created which puts credit within the reach of every man who can show a going business, and the supervision and control of the system is in the hands of a responsible agency of the Government itself. A trade tribunal has been created by which those who attempt unjust and oppressive practices in business can be brought to book. Labor has been made something else in the view of the law than a mercantile commodity—something human and linked with the privileges of life itself. The soil has everywhere been laid bare out of which monopoly is slowly to be eradicated. And undoubtedly the means by which credit has been set free is at the heart of all these things —is the key piece of the whole structure.

. . . The future is clear and bright with promise of the best things. While there was agitation and suspicion and distrust and bitter complaint of wrong, groups and classes were at war with one another, did not see that their interests were common, and suffered only when separated and brought into conflict. Fundamental wrongs once righted, as they may now easily and quickly be, all differences will clear away.

We are all in the same boat, though apparently we have forgotten it. We now know the port for which we are bound. We have and shall have, more and more as our new understandings ripen, a common discipline of patriotic purpose. We shall advance, and advance together, with a new spirit, a new enthusiasm, a new cordiality of spirit and co-operation. It is an inspiring prospect. Our task is henceforth to work, not for any single interest, but for all the interests of the country as a united whole.

The future will be very different from the past, which we shall presently look back upon, I venture to say, as if upon a bad dream. The future will be different in action and different in spirit, a time of healing because a time of just dealing and co-operation between men made equal before the law in fact as well as in name. . . .

During the first phase of the New Freedom program, Wilson, in line with his principle of equal rights for all and special privileges for none, resisted demands for federal intervention in behalf of farmers or laborers. But in 1916— under pressure from more advanced progressives and facing the threat of a reunited Republican party in the upcoming presidential election—he swung to the left and pushed through Congress a new and more far-reaching program of reform. In the following speech of September 2, 1916, accepting the Democratic presidential nomination, he boasts how his administration has enacted into law nearly all of the platform of TR's Progressive party.[3]

. . . Boasting is always an empty business, which pleases nobody but the boaster, and I have no disposition to boast of what the Democratic Party has accomplished. It has merely done its duty. It has merely fulfilled its explicit promises. But there can be no violation of good taste in calling attention to the manner in which those promises have been carried out or in adverting to the interesting fact that many of the things accomplished were what the opposition party had again and again promised to do but had left undone. Indeed that is manifestly part of the business of this year of reckoning and assessment. There is no means of judging the future except by assessing the past. Constructive action must be weighed against destructive comment and reaction. The Democrats either have or have not understood the varied interests of the country. The test is contained in the record.

What is that record? What were the Democrats called into power to do? What things had long waited to be done, and how did the Democrats do them? It is a record of extraordinary length and

[3] Baker and Dodd, eds., *Public Papers of Woodrow Wilson*, IV, 275–81.

variety, rich in elements of many kinds, but consistent in principle throughout and susceptible of brief recital.

The Republican party was put out of power because of failure, practical failure and moral failure; because it had served special interests and not the country at large; because, under the leadership of its preferred and established guides, of those who still make its choices, it had lost touch with the thoughts and the needs of the Nation and was living in a past age and under a fixed illusion of greatness. It had framed tariff laws based upon a fear of foreign trade, a fundamental doubt as to American skill, enterprise, and capacity, and a very tender regard for the profitable privileges of those who had gained control of domestic markets and domestic credits; and yet had enacted antitrust laws which hampered the very things they meant to foster, which were stiff and inelastic, and in part unintelligible. It had permitted the country throughout the long period of its control to stagger from one financial crisis to another under the operation of a national banking law of its own framing which made stringency and panic certain and the control of the larger business operations of the country by the bankers of a few reserve centers inevitable; had made as if it meant to reform the law but had faint-heartedly failed in the attempt, because it could not bring itself to do the one thing necessary to make the reform genuine and effectual, namely, break up the control of small groups of bankers. It had been oblivious, or indifferent, to the fact that the farmers, upon whom the country depends for its food and in the last analysis for its prosperity, were without standing in the matter of commercial credit, without the protection of standards in their market transactions, and without systematic knowledge of the markets themselves; that the labourers of the country, the great army of men who man the industries it was professing to father and promote, carried their labour as a mere commodity to market, were subject to restraint by novel and drastic process in the courts, were without assurance of compensation for industrial accidents, without federal assistance in accommodating labour disputes, and without national aid or advice in finding the places and the industries in which their labour was most needed. The country had no national system of road construction and development. . . .

So things stood when the Democratic Party came into power. How do they stand now? Alike in the domestic field and in the wide field of the commerce of the world, American business and life and industry have been set free to move as they never moved before.

The tariff has been revised, not on the principle of repelling foreign trade, but upon the principle of encouraging it, upon something like a footing of equality with our own in respect of the terms of competition, and a Tariff Board has been created whose function it will be to keep the relations of American with foreign business and industry under constant observation, for the guidance alike of our businessmen and of our Congress. American energies are now directed towards the markets of the world.

The laws against trusts have been clarified by definition, with a view to making it plain that they were not directed against big business but only against unfair business and the pretense of competition where there was none; and a Trade Commission has been created with powers of guidance and accommodation which have relieved business men of unfounded fears and set them upon the road of hopeful and confident enterprise.

By the Federal Reserve Act the supply of currency at the disposal of active business has been rendered elastic, taking its volume, not from a fixed body of investment securities, but from the liquid assets of daily trade; and these assets are assessed and accepted, not by distant groups of bankers in control of unavailable reserves, but by bankers at the many centers of local exchange who are in touch with local conditions everywhere.

Effective measures have been taken for the re-creation of an American merchant marine and the revival of the American carrying trade indispensable to our emancipation from the control which foreigners have so long exercised over the opportunities, the routes, and the methods of our commerce with other countries.

The Interstate Commerce Commission has been reorganized to enable it to perform its great and important functions more promptly and more efficiently. We have created, extended and improved the service of the parcels post.

So much we have done for business. What other party has understood the task so well or executed it so intelligently and energetically? What other party has attempted it at all? The Republican leaders, apparently, know of no means of assisting business but "protection." How to stimulate it and put it upon a new footing of energy and enterprise they have not suggested.

For the farmers of the country we have virtually created commercial credit, by means of the Federal Reserve Act and the Rural Credits Act. They now have the standing of other business men in the money market. We have successfully regulated speculation in "futures" and established standards in the marketing of grains. By an intelligent Warehouse Act we have assisted to make the standard crops available as never before both for systematic marketing and as a security for loans from the banks. We have greatly added to the work of neighborhood demonstration on the farm itself of improved methods of cultivation, and, through the intelligent extension of the functions of the Department of Agriculture, have made it possible for the farmer to learn systematically where his best markets are and how to get at them.

The workingmen of America have been given a veritable emancipation, by the legal recognition of a man's labour as part of his life, and not a mere marketable commodity; by exempting labour organizations from processes of the courts which treated their members like fractional parts of mobs and not like accessible and responsible individuals; by releasing our seamen from involuntary servitude; by making adequate provision for compensation for industrial accidents; by providing suitable machinery for mediation and conciliation in industrial disputes; and by putting the Federal Department of Labor at the disposal of the workingman when in search of work.

We have effected the emancipation of the children of the country by releasing them from hurtful labour. We have instituted a system of national aid in the building of highroads such as the country has been feeling after for a century. We have sought to equalize taxation by means of an equitable income tax. We have taken the steps that ought to have been taken at the outset to open up the resources of Alaska. We have provided for national defense upon a scale never before seriously proposed upon the responsibility of an entire political party. We have driven the tariff lobby from cover and obliged it to substitute solid argument for private influence.

This extraordinary recital must sound like a platform, a list of sanguine promises; but it is not. It is a record of promises made four years ago and now actually redeemed in constructive legislation.

These things must profoundly disturb the thoughts and confound the plans of those who have made themselves believe that the Democratic Party neither understood nor was ready to assist the business of the country in the great enterprises which it is its evident and inevitable destiny to undertake and carry through. The breaking up of the lobby must especially disconcert them; for it was through the lobby that they sought and were sure they had found the heart of things. The game of privilege can be played successfully by no other means.

This record must equally astonish those who feared that the Democratic Party had not opened its heart to comprehend the demands of social justice. We have in four years come very near to carrying out the platform of the Progressive Party as well as our own; for we also are progressives.

There is one circumstance connected with this program which ought to be very plainly stated. It was resisted at every step by the interests which the Republican Party had catered to and fostered at the expense of the country, and these same interests are now earnestly praying for a reaction which will save their privileges—for the restoration of their sworn friends to power before it is too late to recover what they have lost. They fought with particular desperation and infinite resourcefulness the reform of the banking and currency system, knowing that to be the citadel of their control; and most anxiously are they hoping and planning for the amendment of the Federal Reserve Act by the concentration of control in a single bank which the old familiar group of bankers can keep under their eye and direction. But while the "big men" who used to write the tariffs and command the assistance of the Treasury have been hostile—all but a few with vision—the average business man knows that he has been delivered, and that the fear that was once every day in his heart that the men who controlled credit and directed enterprise from the committee rooms of Congress would crush him, is there no more, and will not return—unless the party that consulted only the "big men" should return to power—the party of masterly inactivity and cunning resourcefulness in standing pat to resist change. . . .

MISSIONARY DIPLOMACY

Wilson insisted that American diplomacy should be guided by moral precepts free from any taint of selfish aggrandizement. But his commitment to preserving American supremacy in Central America and the Caribbean in order to protect the Panama Canal coupled with his missionary zeal to train the Latin Americans in good citizenship—Anglo-Saxon style—led the United States into unparalled diplomatic and military interference south of the border. The worst trouble spot was Mexico. And the first step into the Mexican morass was Wilson's determination—expressed in this circular letter to the powers of November 24, 1913—to topple Mexican dictator Victoriano Huerta.[4]

The purpose of the United States is solely and singly to secure peace and order in Central America by seeing to it that the processes of self-government there are not interrupted or set aside.

Usurpations like that of General Huerta menace the peace and development of America as nothing else could. They not only render the development of ordered self-government impossible: they also tend to set law entirely aside, to put the lives and fortunes of citizens and foreigners alike in constant jeopardy, to invalidate contracts and concessions in any way the usurper may devise for his own profit, and to impair both the national credit and all the foundations of business, domestic or foreign.

It is the purpose of the United States, therefore, to discredit and defeat such usurpations whenever they occur. The present policy of the Government of the United States is to isolate General Huerta entirely; to cut him off from foreign sympathy and aid and from domestic credit, whether moral or material, and so to force him out.

It hopes and believes that isolation will accomplish this end, and shall await the results without irritation or impatience. If General Huerta does not retire by force of circumstances, it will become the

---

[4] Selection from Arthur S. Link, *Wilson: The New Freedom* (Princeton: Princeton University Press, 1956), Vol. II, 386–87. (Copyright © 1956 by Princeton University Press; Princeton Paperback, 1967.) Reprinted by permission of Princeton University Press.

duty of the United States to use less peaceful means to put him out. It will give other governments notice in advance of each affirmative or aggressive step it has in contemplation, should it unhappily become necessary to move actively against the usurper; but no such step seems immediately necessary.

Its fixed resolve is, that no such interruptions of civil order shall be tolerated so far as it is concerned. Each conspicuous instance in which usurpations of this kind are prevented will render their recurrence less likely, and in the end a state of affairs will be secured in Mexico and elsewhere upon this continent which will assure the peace of America and the untrammeled development of its economic and social relations with the rest of the world.

Beyond this fixed purpose the Government of the United States will not go. It will not permit itself to seek any special or exclusive advantages in Mexico or elsewhere for its own citizens, but will seek, here as elsewhere, to show itself the consistent champion of the open door. . . .

> *Wilson succeeded in overthrowing Huerta. But the civil strife and turmoil that followed in the wake of his downfall led the American chief executive to issue the following warning on June 2, 1915, thus setting the stage for General John J. Pershing's frustrating and embarrassing punitive expedition of 1916–17 that brought the two countries to the verge of war.*[5]

For more than two years revolutionary conditions have existed in Mexico. The purpose of the revolution was to rid Mexico of men who ignored the constitution of the Republic and used their power in contempt of the rights of its people; and with these purposes the people of the United States instinctively and generously sympathized. But the leaders of the revolution, in the very hour of their success, have disagreed and turned their arms against one another. All professing the same objects, they are nevertheless unable or unwilling to co-operate. A central authority at Mexico City is no sooner set up than it is undermined and its authority

[5] Baker and Dodd, eds., *Public Papers of Woodrow Wilson*, III, 339–40.

denied by those who were expected to support it. Mexico is apparently no nearer a solution of her tragical troubles than she was when the revolution was first kindled. And she has been swept by civil war as if by fire. Her crops are destroyed, her fields lie unseeded, her work cattle are confiscated for the use of the armed factions, her people flee to the mountains to escape being drawn into unavailing bloodshed, and no man seems to see or lead the way to peace and settled order. There is no proper protection either for her own citizens or for the citizens of other nations resident and at work within her territory. Mexico is starving and without a government.

In these circumstances the people and Government of the United States cannot stand indifferently by and do nothing to serve their neighbor. They want nothing for themselves in Mexico. Least of all do they desire to settle her affairs for her, or claim any right to do so. But neither do they wish to see utter ruin come upon her, and they deem it their duty as friends and neighbors to lend any aid they properly can to any instrumentality which promises to be effective in bringing about a settlement which will embody the real objects of the revolution—constitutional government and the rights of the people. Patriotic Mexicans are sick at heart and cry out for peace and for every self-sacrifice that may be necessary to procure it. Their people cry out for food and will presently hate as much as they fear every man, in their country or out of it, who stands between them and their daily bread.

It is time, therefore, that the Government of the United States should frankly state the policy which in these extraordinary circumstances it becomes its duty to adopt. It must presently do what it has not hitherto done or felt at liberty to do, lend its active moral support to some man or group of men, if such may be found, who can rally the suffering people of Mexico to their support in an effort to ignore, if they cannot unite, the warring factions of the country, return to the constitution of the Republic so long in abeyance, and set up a government at Mexico City which the great powers of the world can recognize and deal with, a government with which the program of the revolution will be a business and not merely a platform. I, therefore, publicly and very solemnly, call upon the leaders of faction in Mexico to act, to act together, and to act promptly for the relief and redemption of their prostrate country. I feel it to be my duty to tell them that, if they cannot accommodate their differences and unite for this great purpose within a very short time, this Government will be constrained to decide what means should be employed by the United States in order to help Mexico save herself and serve her people.

FROM NEUTRALITY TO WAR

Although Wilson urged the American people immediately after the outbreak of hostilities in Europe to remain neutral in thought as well as deed, he himself failed to live up to his own words. While he repeatedly protested British violations of neutral rights, he never took as strong a stand against Britain's naval measures as he did against German submarine warfare in the following instructions of February 10, 1915, to the American ambassador to Germany, James W. Gerard.[6]

Please address a note immediately to the Imperial German Government to the following effect:

The Government of the United States, having had its attention directed to the proclamation of the German Admiralty issued on the fourth of February, that the waters surrounding Great Britain and Ireland, including the whole of the English Channel, are to be considered as comprised within the seat of war; that all enemy merchant vessels found in those waters after the eighteenth instant will be destroyed, although it may not always be possible to save crews and passengers; and that neutral vessels expose themselves to danger within this zone of war because, in view of the misuse of neutral flags said to have been ordered by the British Government on the thirty-first of January and of the contingencies of maritime warfare, it may not be possible always to exempt neutral vessels from attacks intended to strike enemy ships, feels it to be its duty to call the attention of the Imperial German Government, with sincere respect and the most friendly sentiments but very candidly and earnestly, to the very serious possibilities of the course of action apparently contemplated under that proclamation.

The Government of the United States views those possibilities

6 Baker and Dodd, eds., *Public Papers of Woodrow Wilson*, III, 280–83.

with such grave concern that it feels it to be its privilege, and indeed its duty in the circumstances, to request the Imperial German Government to consider before action is taken the critical situation in respect of the relations between this country and Germany which might arise were the German naval forces, in carrying out the policy foreshadowed in the Admiralty's proclamation, to destroy any merchant vessel of the United States or cause the death of American citizens.

It is of course not necessary to remind the German Government that the sole right of a belligerent in dealing with neutral vessels on the high seas is limited to visit and search, unless a blockade is proclaimed and effectively maintained, which this Government does not understand to be proposed in this case. To declare or exercise a right to attack and destroy any vessel entering a prescribed area of the high seas without first certainly determining it belligerent nationality and the contraband character of its cargo would be an act so unprecedented in naval warfare that this Government is reluctant to believe that the Imperial Government of Germany in this case contemplates it as possible. The suspicion that enemy ships are using neutral flags improperly can create no just presumption that all ships traversing a prescribed area are subject to the same suspicion. It is to determine exactly such questions that this Government understands the right of visit and search to have been recognized.

This Government has carefully noted the explanatory statement issued by the Imperial German Government at the same time with the proclamation of the German Admiralty, and takes this occasion to remind the Imperial German Government very respectfully that the Government of the United States is open to none of the criticisms for unneutral action to which the German Government believe the governments of certain of other neutral nations have laid themselves open; that the Government of the United States has not consented to or acquiesced in any measures which may have been taken by the other belligerent nations in the present war which operate to restrain neutral trade, but has, on the contrary, taken in all such matters a position which warrants it in holding those governments responsible in the proper way for any untoward effects upon American shipping which the accepted principles of international law do not justify; and that it, therefore, regards itself as free in the present instance to take with a clear conscience and upon accepted principles the position indicated in this note.

If the commanders of German vessels of war should act upon the presumption that the flag of the United States was not being used in good faith and should destroy on the high seas an American vessel or the lives of American citizens, it would be difficult for the Government of the United States to view the act in any other light than as an indefensible violation of neutral rights which it would be very hard indeed to reconcile with the friendly relations now so happily subsisting between the two Governments.

If such a deplorable situation should arise, the imperial German Government can readily appreciate that the Government of the United States would be constrained to hold the Imperial German Government to a strict accountability for such acts of their naval authorities and to take any steps it might be necessary to take to safeguard American lives and property and to secure to American citizens the full enjoyment of their acknowledged rights on the high seas.

The Government of the United States, in view of these considerations, which it urges with the greatest respect and with the sincere purpose of making sure that no misunderstanding may arise and no circumstance occur that might even cloud the intercourse of the two Governments, expresses the confident hope and expectation that the Imperial German Government can and will give assurance that American citizens and their vessels will not be molested by the naval forces of Germany otherwise than by visit and search, though their vessels may be traversing the sea area delimited in the proclamation of the German Admiralty. . . .

Wilson explains his rationale for the contrast between his acquiescence to British naval measures and his insistence upon holding Germany to strict accountability on the submarine issue in this note of June 2, 1915, to Secretary of State William Jennings Bryan.[7]

[7] U.S. State Department, *Papers Relating to the Foreign Relations of the United States: The Lansing Papers, 1914–1920* (Washington, D.C.: Government Printing Office, 1939–40), I, 421.

It is interesting and significant how often the German Foreign Office goes over the same ground in different words, and always misses the essential point involved, that England's violation of neutral rights is different from Germany's violation of the rights of humanity.

When Democratic members of Congress, worried about the danger of the United States entering the war against Germany in defense of the right of American citizens to travel on belligerent merchantmen, sought to pass the Gore-Mc-Lemore resolutions warning against such travel, Wilson intervened decisively with this letter of February 24, 1916, to Senator William J. Stone of Missouri, the chairman of the Senate Foreign Relations Committee, to block their adoption.[8]

. . . You are right in assuming that I shall do everything in my power to keep the United States out of war. I think the country will feel no uneasiness about my course in that respect. Through many anxious months I have striven for that object, amidst difficulties more manifold than can have been apparent upon the surface; and so far I have succeeded. I do not doubt that I shall continue to succeed. The course which the central European powers have announced their intention of following in the future with regard to undersea warfare seems for the moment to threaten insuperable obstacles, but its apparent meaning is so manifestly inconsistent with explicit assurances recently given us by those powers with regard to their treatment of merchant vessels on the high seas that I must believe that explanations will presently ensue which will put a different aspect upon it. We have had no reason to question their good faith or their fidelity to their promises in the past, and I, for one, feel confident that we shall have none in the future.

But in any event our duty is clear. No nation, no group of nations, has the right while war is in progress to alter or disregard the principles which all nations have agreed upon in mitigation of the horrors and sufferings of war; and if the clear rights of American citizens should ever unhappily be abridged or denied by any

[8] Baker and Dodd, eds., *Public Papers of Woodrow Wilson*, IV, 122–23.

such action, we should, it seems to me, have in honor no choice as to what our own course should be.

For my own part, I can not consent to any abridgment of the rights of American citizens in any respect. The honor and self-respect of the nation is involved. We covet peace, and shall preserve it at any cost but the loss of honor. To forbid our people to exercise their rights for fear we might be called upon to vindicate them would be a deep humiliation indeed. It would be an implicit, all but an explicit, acquiescence in the violation of the rights of mankind everywhere and of whatever nation or allegiance. It would be a deliberate abdication of our hitherto proud position as spokesmen even amidst the turmoil of war for the law and the right. It would make everything this Government has attempted and everything that it has achieved during this terrible struggle of nations meaningless and futile.

It is important to reflect that if in this instance we allowed expediency to take the place of principle, the door would inevitably be opened to still further concessions. Once accept a single abatement of right and many other humiliations would certainly follow, and the whole fine fabric of international law might crumble under our hands piece by piece. What we are contending for in this matter is of the very essence of the things that have made America a sovereign nation. She cannot yield them without conceding her own impotency as a nation and making virtual surrender of her independent position among the nations of the world. . . .

Although Wilson succeeded in temporarily forcing Germany to back down, his adamant stand left him no alternative except to ask Congress for a declaration of war when Germany resumed its unrestricted submarine warfare. But in his war message of April 2, 1917, Wilson seeks to justify United States involvement in terms broader and more noble than the simple defense of American neutral rights.[9]

I have called the Congress into extraordinary session because there are serious, very serious, choices of policy to be made, and

---

[9] *Congressional Record,* Special Session and 65th Cong., 1st sess., LV (1917), pt. 1, 102–4.

made immediately, which it was neither right nor constitutionally permissible that I should assume the responsibility of making.

On the third of February last I officially laid before you the extraordinary announcement of the Imperial German Government that on and after the first day of February it was its purpose to put aside all restraints of law or of humanity and use its submarines to sink every vessel that sought to approach either the ports of Great Britain and Ireland or the western coasts of Europe or any of the ports controlled by the enemies of Germany within the Mediterranean. That had seemed to be the object of the German submarine warfare earlier in the war, but since April of last year the Imperial Government had somewhat restrained the commanders of its undersea craft in conformity with its promise then given to us that passenger boats should not be sunk and that due warning would be given to all other vessels which its submarines might seek to destroy, when no resistance was offered or escape attempted, and care taken that their crews were given at least a fair chance to save their lives in their open boats. The precautions taken were meagre and haphazard enough, as was proved in distressing instance after instance in the progress of the cruel and unmanly business, but a certain degree of restraint was observed. The new policy has swept every restriction aside. Vessels of every kind, whatever their flag, their character, their cargo, their destination, their errand, have been ruthlessly sent to the bottom without warning and without thought of help or mercy for those on board, the vessels of friendly neutrals along with those of belligerents. Even hospital ships and ships carrying relief to the sorely bereaved and stricken people of Belgium, though the latter were provided with safe conduct through the proscribed areas by the German Government itself and were distinguished by unmistakable marks of identity, have been sunk with the same reckless lack of compassion or of principle.

I was for a little while unable to believe that such things would in fact be done by any government that had hitherto subscribed to the humane practices of civilized nations. International law had its origin in the attempt to set up some law which would be respected and observed upon the seas, where no nation had right of dominion and where lay the free highways of the world. By painful stage after stage has that law been built up, with meagre enough results, indeed, after all was accomplished that could be accomplished, but always with a clear view, at least, of what the heart and conscience of mankind demanded. This minimum of right the German Government has swept aside under the plea of retaliation and necessity and because it had no weapons which it could use at sea except these which it is impossible to employ as it is employing them without throwing to the winds all scruples of humanity or of respect for the understandings that were supposed to underlie the intercourse of the world. I am not now thinking of the loss of property involved, immense and serious as that is, but only of the wanton and wholesale destruction of the lives of noncombatants, men, women, and children, engaged in pursuits which have always, even in the darkest periods of modern history, been deemed innocent and legitimate. Property can be paid for; the lives of peaceful and innocent people cannot be. The present German submarine warfare against commerce is a warfare against mankind.

It is a war against all nations. American ships have been sunk, American lives taken, in ways which it has stirred us very deeply to learn of, but the ships and people of other neutral and friendly nations have been sunk and overwhelmed in the waters in the same way. There has been no discrimination. The challenge is to all mankind. Each nation must decide for itself how it will meet it. The choice we make for ourselves must be made with a moderation of counsel and a temperateness of judgment befitting our character and our motives as a nation. We must put excited feeling away. Our motive will not be revenge or the victorious assertion of the physical might of the nation, but only the vindication of right, of human right, of which we are only a single champion.

When I addressed the Congress on the twenty-sixth of February last I thought that it would suffice to assert our neutral rights with arms, our right to use the seas against unlawful interference, our right to keep our people safe against unlawful violence. But armed neutrality, it now appears, is impracticable. Because submarines are in effect outlaws when used as the German submarines have been used against merchant shipping, it is impossible to defend ships against their attacks as the law of nations has assumed that merchantmen would defend themselves against privateers or cruisers, visible craft giving chase upon the open sea. It is common prudence in such circumstances, grim necessity indeed, to endeavour to destroy them before they have shown their own intention. They must be dealt with upon sight, if dealt with at all. The German Government denies the right of neutrals to use arms at all within the areas of the sea which it has proscribed, even in the defense of rights which no modern publicist has ever before questioned their right to defend. The intimation is conveyed that the armed guards which we have placed on our merchant ships will be treated as beyond the pale of law and subject to be dealt with as pirates would be. Armed neutrality is ineffectual enough at best; in such circumstances and in the fact of such pretensions it is worse than ineffectual: it is likely only to produce what it was meant to prevent; it is practically certain to draw us into the war without either the rights or the effectiveness of belligerents. There is one choice we cannot make, we are incapable of making: we will not choose the path of submission and suffer the most sacred rights of our Nation and our people to be ignored or violated. The wrongs against which we now array ourselves are no common wrongs; they cut to the very roots of human life.

With a profound sense of the solemn and even tragical character of the step I am taking and of the grave responsibilities which it involves, but in unhesitating obedience to what I deem my constitutional duty, I advise that the Congress declare the recent course of the Imperial German Government to be in fact nothing less than war against the Government and people of the United States; that it formally accept the status of belligerent which has thus been thrust upon it; and that it take immediate steps not only to put the country in a more thorough state of defense but also to exert all its power and employ all its resources to bring the Government of the German Empire to terms and end the war. . . .

. . . Let us be very clear, and make very clear to all the world what our motives and our objects are. . . . Our object . . . is to vindicate the principles of peace and justice in the life of the world as against selfish and autocratic power and to set up amongst the really free and self-governed peoples of the world such a concert of purpose and of action as will henceforth insure the observance of those principles. Neutrality is no longer feasible or desirable where the peace of the world is involved and the freedom of its peoples, and the menace to that peace and freedom lies in the existence of autocratic governments backed by organized force which is controlled wholly by their will, not by the will of their people. We have seen the last of neutrality in such circumstances. We are at the beginning of an age in which it will be insisted that the same standards of conduct and of responsibility for wrong done shall be observed among nations and their governments that are observed among the individual citizens of civilized states. . . .

. . . We are now about to accept gage of battle with this natural foe to liberty and shall, if necessary, spend the whole force of the Nation to check and nullify its pretensions and its power. We are glad now that we see the facts with no veil of false pretense about them, to fight thus for the ultimate peace of the world and for the liberation of its peoples . . . : for the rights of nations great and small and the privilege of men everywhere to choose their way of life and of obedience. The world must be made safe for democracy. Its peace must be planted upon the tested foundations of political liberty. We have no selfish ends to serve. We desire no conquest, no dominion. We seek no indemnities for ourselves, no material compensation for the sacrifices we shall freely make. We are but one of the champions of the right of mankind. We shall be satisfied when those rights have been made as secure as the faith and the freedom of nations can make them. . . .

It is a distressing and oppressive duty, Gentlemen of the Congress, which I have performed in thus addressing you. There are, it may be, many months of fiery trial and sacrifice ahead of us. It is a fearful thing to lead this great peaceful people into war, into the most terrible and disastrous of all wars, civilization itself seeming to be in the balance. But the right is more precious than peace, and we shall fight for the things which we have always carried nearest our hearts—for democracy, for the right of those who submit to authority to have a voice in their own Governments, for the rights and liberties of small nations, for a universal dominion of right by such a concert of free peoples as shall bring peace and safety to all nations and make the world itself at last free. To such a task we can dedicate our lives and our fortunes, everything that we are and everything that we have, with the pride of those who know that the day has come when America is privileged to spend her blood and her might for the principles that gave her birth and happiness and the peace which she has treasured. God helping her, she can do no other.

A JUST AND LASTING PEACE

Wilson first began to think seriously about a postwar collective security organization to maintain the peace in 1916 as part of his unsuccessful mediation efforts. Setting forth his war aims in his January 8, 1918, address to Congress—the famous Fourteen Points—he makes the establishment of a League of Nations the keystone of his hopes for a just and lasting peace.[10]

. . . No statesman who has the least conception of his responsibility ought for a moment to permit himself to continue this tragical and appalling outpouring of blood and treasure unless he is sure beyond a peradventure that the objects of the vital sacrifice are part and parcel of the very life of Society and that the people for whom he speaks think them right and imperative as he does. . . .

It will be our wish and purpose that the processes of peace, when they are begun, shall be absolutely open and that they shall involve and permit henceforth no secret understandings of any kind. The day of conquest and aggrandizement is gone by; so is also the day of secret covenants entered into in the interest of particular governments and likely at some unlooked-for moment to upset the peace of the world. . . .

We entered this war because violations of right had occurred which touched us to the quick and made the life of our own people impossible unless they were corrected and the world secured once for all against their recurrence. What we demand in this war, therefore, is nothing peculiar to ourselves. It is that the world be made fit and safe to live in; and particularly that it be made safe for every peace-loving nation which, like our own, wishes to live its own life, determine its own institutions, be assured of justice and fair dealing by the other peoples of the world as against force and selfish aggression. All the peoples of the world are in effect partners in this interest, and for our own part we see very clearly

[10] *Congressional Record*, 65th Cong., 2nd sess., LVI (1917–18), pt. 1, 680–81.

that unless justice be done to others it will not be done to us. The programme of the world's peace, therefore, is our programme, and that programme, the only possible programme, as we see it, is this:

I. Open covenants of peace, openly arrived at, after which there shall be no private international understandings of any kind but diplomacy shall proceed always frankly and in the public view.

II. Absolute freedom of navigation upon the seas, outside territorial waters, alike in peace and in war, except as the seas may be closed in whole or in part by international action for the enforcement of international covenants.

III. The removal, so far as possible, of all economic barriers and the establishment of an equality of trade conditions among all the nations consenting to the peace and associating themselves for its maintenance.

IV. Adequate guarantees given and taken that national armaments will be reduced to the lowest point consistent with domestic safety.

V. A free, open-minded, and absolutely impartial adjustment of all colonial claims, based upon a strict observance of the principle that in determining all such questions of sovereignty the interests of the populations concerned must have equal weight with the equitable claims of the government whose title is to be determined.

VI. The evacuation of all Russian territory and such a settlement of all questions affecting Russia as will secure the best and freest cooperation of the other nations of the world in obtaining for her an unhampered and unembarrassed opportunity for the independent determination of her own political development and national policy and assure her of a sincere welcome into the society of free nations under institutions of her own choosing; and, more than a welcome, assistance also of every kind that she may need and may herself desire. The treatment accorded Russia by her sister nations in the months to come will be the acid test of their good will, of their comprehension of her needs as distinguished from their own interests, and of their intelligent and unselfish sympathy.

VII. Belgium, the whole world will agree, must be evacuated and restored, without any attempt to limit the sovereignty which she enjoys in common with all other free nations. No other single act will serve as this will serve to restore confidence among the nations in the laws which they have themselves set and determined for the government of their relations with one another. Without this healing act the whole structure and validity of international law is forever impaired.

VIII. All French territory should be freed and the invaded portions restored, and the wrong done to France by Prussia in 1871 in the matter of Alsace-Lorraine, which has unsettled the peace of the world for nearly fifty years, should be righted, in order that peace may once more be made secure in the interest of all.

IX. A readjustment of the frontiers of Italy should be effected along clearly recognizable lines of nationality.

X. The peoples of Austria-Hungary, whose place among the nations we wish to see safeguarded and assured, should be accorded the freest opportunity of autonomous development.

XI. Rumania, Serbia, and Montenegro should be evacuated; occupied territories restored; Serbia accorded free and secure access to the sea; and the relations of the several Balkan states to one another determined by friendly counsel along historically established lines of allegiance and nationality; and international guarantees of the political and economic independence and territorial integrity of the several Balkan states should be entered into.

XII. The Turkish portions of the present Ottoman Empire should be assured a secure sovereignty, but the other nationalities which are now under Turkish rule should be assured an undoubted security of life and an absolutely unmolested opportunity of autonomous development, and the Dardanelles should be permanently opened as a free passage to the ships and commerce of all nations under international guarantees.

XIII. An independent Polish state should be erected which should include the territories inhabited by indisputably Polish populations, which should be assured a free and secure access to the sea, and whose political and economic independence and territorial integrity should be guaranteed by international covenant.

XIV. A general association of nations must be formed under specific covenants for the purpose of affording mutual guarantees of political independence and territorial integrity to great and small states alike.

In regard to these essential rectifications of wrong and assertions of right we feel ourselves to be intimate partners of all the governments and peoples associated together against the Imperialists. We cannot be separated in interest or divided in purpose. We stand together until the end.

For such arrangements and covenants we are willing to fight and to continue to fight until they are achieved; but only because we wish the right to prevail and desire a just and stable peace such as can be secured only by removing the chief provocations to war, which this programme does remove. We have no jealousy of German greatness, and there is nothing in this programme that impairs it. We grudge her no achievement or distinction of learning or of pacific enterprise such as have made her record very bright and very enviable. We do not wish to injure her or to block in any way her legitimate influence or power. We do not wish to fight her either with arms or with hostile arrangements of trade if she is willing to associate herself with us and the other peace-loving nations of the world in covenants of justice and law and fair dealing. We wish her only to accept a place of equality among the peoples of the world—the new world in which we now live—instead of a place of mastery.

Neither do we presume to suggest to her any alteration or modification of her institutions. But it is necessary, we must frankly say, and necessary as a preliminary to any intelligent dealings with her on our part, that we should know whom her spokesmen speak for when they speak to us, whether for the Reichstag majority or for the military party and the men whose creed is imperial domination.

We have spoken now, surely, in terms too concrete to admit of any further doubt or question. An evident principle runs through the whole program I have outlined. It is the principle of justice to all peoples and nationalities, and their right to live on equal terms of liberty and safety with one another, whether they be strong or weak. Unless this principle be made its foundation no part of the structure of international justice can stand. The people of the United States could act upon no other principle; and to the vindication of this principle they are ready to devote their lives, their honor, and everything that they possess. The moral climax of this the culminating and final war for human liberty has come, and they are ready to put their own strength, their own highest purpose, their own integrity and devotion to the test.

*Wilson was successful in winning approval of the League
of Nations from the powers at the Paris Peace Conference.
But upon his return home he found growing opposition to
the Versailles treaty and American membership in the League.
In response, Wilson decided to pressure the Senate by appealing directly to the people. Perhaps his most effective defense of the treaty was in this speech at Pueblo, Colorado,
September 25, 1919, just before his physical collapse ending
his leadership in the fight to save the treaty.*[11]

. . . I have perceived more and more that men have been
busy creating an absolutely false impression of what the treaty of
peace and the Covenant of the League of Nations contain and mean.
I find, moreover, that there is an organized propaganda against the
League of Nations and against the treaty proceeding from exactly
the same sources that the organized propaganda proceeded from
which threatened this country here and there with disloyalty, and
I want to say—I cannot say too often—any man who carries a
hyphen about with him carries a dagger that he is ready to plunge
into the vitals of this Republic whenever he gets ready. If I can
catch any man with a hyphen in this great contest I will know that
I have got an enemy of the Republic. My fellow citizens, it is only
certain bodies of foreign sympathies, certain bodies of sympathy
with foreign nations that are organized against this great document
which the American representatives have brought back from Paris.
Therefore, in order to clear away the mists, in order to remove the
impressions, in order to check the falsehoods that have clustered
around this great subject, I want to tell you a few very simple
things about the treaty and the Covenant.

Do not think of this treaty of peace as merely a settlement with
Germany. It is that. It is a very severe settlement with Germany,
but there is not anything in it that she did not earn. Indeed, she
earned more than she can ever be able to pay for, and the punishment exacted of her is not a punishment greater than she can bear,
and it is absolutely necessary in order that no other nation may ever
plot such a thing against humanity and civilization. But the treaty

[11] Baker and Dodd, eds., *Public Papers of Woodrow Wilson*, VI, 399–413, 415–
16.

is so much more than that. It is not merely a settlement with Germany; it is a readjustment of those great injustices which underlie the whole structure of European and Asiatic society. This is only the first of several treaties. They are all constructed upon the same plan. . . . They are based upon the purpose to see that every government dealt with in this great settlement is put in the hands of the people and taken out of the hands of coteries and of sovereigns who had no right to rule over the people. It is a people's treaty, that accomplishes by a great sweep of practical justice the liberation of men who never could have liberated themselves, and the power of the most powerful nations has been devoted not to their aggrandizement but to the liberation of people whom they could have put under their control if they had chosen to do so. Not one foot of territory is demanded by the conquerors, not one single item of submission to their authority is demanded by them. The men who sat around that table in Paris knew that the time had come when the people were no longer going to consent to live under masters, but were going to live the lives that they chose themselves, to live under such governments as they chose themselves to erect. That is the fundamental principle of this great settlement. . . .

At the front of this great treaty is put the Covenant of the League of Nations. . . . Unless you get the united, concerted purpose and power of the great Governments of the world behind this settlement, it will fall down like a house of cards. There is only one power to put behind the liberation of mankind, and that is the power of mankind. It is the power of the united moral forces of the world, and in the Covenant of the League of Nations the moral forces of the world are mobilized. For what purpose? Reflect, my fellow citizens, that the membership of this great League is going to include all the great fighting nations of the world, as well as the weak ones. It is not for the present going to include Germany, but for the time being Germany is not a great fighting country. All the nations that have power that can be mobilized are going to be members of this League, including the United States. And what do they unite for? They enter into a solemn promise to one another that they will never use their power against one another for aggression; that they never will impair the territorial integrity of a neighbor; that they never will interfere with the political independence of a neighbor; that they will abide by the principle that great populations are entitled to determine their own destiny and that they will not interfere with that destiny; and that no matter what differences arise amongst them they will never resort to war without first having done one or other of two things—either submitted the matter of controversy to arbitration, in which case they agree to abide by the result without question, or submitted it to the consideration of the council of the League of Nations, laying before that council all the documents, all the facts, agreeing that the council can publish the documents and the facts to the whole world, agreeing that there shall be six months allowed for the mature consideration of those facts by the council, and agreeing that at the expiration of the six months, even if they are not then ready to accept the advice of the council with regard to the settlement of the dispute, they will still not go to war for another three months. In other words, they consent, no matter what happens, to submit every matter of difference between them to the judgment of mankind, and just so certainly as they do that, my fellow citizens, war will be in the far background, war will be pushed out of that foreground of terror in which it has kept the world for generation after generation, and men will know that there will be a calm time of deliberate counsel. The most dangerous thing for a bad cause is to expose it to the opinion of the world. The most certain way that you can prove that a man is mistaken is by letting all his neighbors know what he thinks, by letting all his neighbors discuss what he thinks, and if he is in the wrong you will notice that he will stay at home, he will not walk on the street. He will be afraid of the eyes of his neighbors. He will be afraid of their judgment of his character. He will know that his cause is lost unless he can sustain it by the arguments of right and of justice. The same law that applies to individuals applies to nations.

But, you say, "We have heard that we might be at a disadvantage in the League of Nations." Well, whoever told you that either was deliberately falsifying or he had not read the Covenant of the League of Nations. I leave him the choice. I want to give you a very simple account of the organization of the League of Nations and let you judge for yourselves. It is a very simple organization. The power of the League, or rather the activities of the League, lie in two bodies. There is the council, which consists of one representative from each of the principal allied and associated powers—that is to say, the United States, Great Britain, France, Italy, and Japan, along with four other representatives of smaller powers chosen out of the general body of the membership of the League. The council is the source of every active policy of the League, and no active policy of the League can be adopted without a unanimous vote of the council. That is explicitly stated in the Covenant itself. Does it not evidently follow that the League of Nations can adopt no policy whatever without the consent of the United States? The affirmative vote of the representative of the United States is necessary in every case. Now, you have heard of six votes belonging to the British Empire. Those six votes are not in the council. They are in the assembly, and the interesting thing is that the assembly does not vote. I must qualify that statement a little, but essentially it is absolutely true. In every matter in which the assembly is given a voice, and there are only four or five, its vote does not count unless concurred in by the representatives of all the nations represented on the council, so that there is no validity to any vote of the assembly unless in that vote also the representative of the United States concurs. That one vote of the United States is as big as the six votes of the British Empire. I am not jealous for advantage, my fellow citizens, but I think that is a perfectly safe situation. There is no validity in a vote, either by the council or the assembly, in which we do not concur. So much for the statements about the six votes of the British Empire.

Look at it in another aspect. The assembly is the talking body. The assembly was created in order that anybody that purposed anything wrong should be subjected to the awkward circumstance that everybody could talk about it. This is the great assembly in which all the things that are likely to disturb the peace of the world or the good understanding between nations are to be exposed to the general view, and I want to ask you if you think it was unjust, unjust to the United States, that speaking parts should be assigned to the several portions of the British Empire? . . . Those speaking parts cannot translate themselves into five votes that can in any matter override the voice and purpose of the United States. . . .

When you come to the heart of the Covenant, my fellow citizens, you will find it in Article X, and I am very much interested to know that the other things have been blown away like bubbles. There is nothing in the other contentions with regard to the League of

Nations, but there is something in Article X that you ought to realize and ought to accept or reject. Article X is the heart of the whole matter. What is Article X? I never am certain that I can from memory give a literal repetition of its language, but I am sure that I can give an exact interpretation of its meaning. Article X provides that every member of the League covenants to respect and preserve the territorial integrity and existing political independence of every other member of the League as against external aggression. Not against internal disturbance. There was not a man at that table who did not admit the sacredness of the right of self-determination, the sacredness of the right of any body of people to say that they would not continue to live under the Government they were then living under, and under Article XI of the Covenant they are given a place to say whether they will live under it or not. For following Article X is Article XI, which makes it the right of any member of the League at any time to call attention to anything, anywhere, that is likely to disturb the peace of the world or the good understanding between nations upon which the peace of the world depends. I want to give you an illustration of what that would mean.

You have heard a great deal—something that was true and a great deal that was false—about that provision of the treaty which hands over to Japan the rights which Germany enjoyed in the Province of Shantung in China. In the first place, Germany did not enjoy any rights there that other nations had not already claimed. For my part, my judgment, my moral judgment, is against the whole set of concessions. They were all of them unjust to China, they ought never to have been exacted, they were all exacted by duress, from a great body of thoughtful and ancient and helpless people. There never was any right in any of them. Thank God, America never asked for any, never dreamed of asking for any. But when Germany got this concession in 1898, the Government of the United States made no protest whatever . . . because the state of international law at that time was that it was none of their business unless they could show that the interests of the United States were affected, and the only thing that they could show with regard to the interests of the United States was that Germany might close the doors of Shantung Province against the trade of the United States. They, therefore, demanded and obtained promises that we could continue to sell merchandise in Shantung. Immediately following that concession to Germany there was a concession to Russia of the same sort, of Port Arthur, and Port Arthur was handed over subsequently to Japan . . . by a treaty written at Portsmouth, N. H., . . . without the slightest intimation from any authoritative sources in America that the Government of the United States had any objection. . . . Now, read Articles X and XI. You will see that international law is revolutionized by putting morals into it. Article X says that no member of the League, and that includes all these nations that have demanded these things unjustly of China, shall impair the territorial integrity or the political independence of any other member of the League. China is going to be a member of the League. Article XI says that any member of the League can call attention to anything that is likely to disturb the peace of the world or the good understanding between nations, and China is for the first time in the history of mankind afforded a standing before the jury of the world. I, for my part, have a profound sympathy for China, and I am proud to have taken part in an arrangement which promises the protection of the world to the rights of China. The whole atmosphere of the world is changed by a thing like that, my fellow citizens. The whole international practice of the world is revolutionized.

But you will say, "What is the second sentence of Article X? That is what gives very disturbing thoughts." The second sentence is that the council of the League shall advise what steps, if any, are necessary to carry out the guarantee of the first sentence, namely, that the members will respect and preserve the territorial integrity and political independence of the other members. I do not know any other meaning for the word "advise" except "advise." The council advises, and it cannot advise without the vote of the United States. Why gentlemen should fear that the Congress of the United States would be advised to do something that it did not want to do I frankly cannot imagine, because they cannot even be advised to do anything unless their own representative has participated in the advice. It may be that that will impair somewhat the vigor of the League, but, nevertheless, the fact is so, that we are not obliged to take any advice except our own, which to any man who wants to go his own course is a very satisfactory state of affairs. Every man regards his own advice as best, and I dare say every man mixes his own advice with some thought of his own interest. Whether we use it wisely or unwisely, we can use the vote of the United States to make impossible drawing the United States into any enterprise that she does not care to be drawn into.

Yet Article X strikes at the taproot of war. Article X is a statement that the very things that have always been sought in imperialistic wars are henceforth forgone by every ambitious nation in the world. . . .

. . . The Covenant in another portion guarantees to the members the independent control of their domestic questions. There is not a leg for these gentlemen to stand on when they say that the interests of the United States are not safeguarded in the very points where we are most sensitive. You do not need to be told again that the Covenant expressly says that nothing in this Covenant shall be construed as affecting the validity of the Monroe Doctrine, for example. You could not be more explicit than that. . . .

. . . We have got to do one or other of two things—we have got to adopt it or reject it. There is no middle course. You cannot go in on a special-privilege basis of your own. I take it that you are too proud to ask to be exempted from responsibilities which the other members of the League will carry. We go in upon equal terms or we do not go in at all; and if we do not go in, my fellow citizens, think of the tragedy of that result—the only sufficient guarantee to the peace of the world withheld! Ourselves drawn apart with that dangerous pride which means that we shall be ready to take care of ourselves, and that means that we shall maintain great standing armies and an irresistible navy; that means we shall have the organization of a military nation; that means we shall have a general staff, with the kind of power that the general staff of Germany had; to mobilize this great manhood of the Nation when it pleases, all the energy of our young men drawn into the thought and preparation for war. What of our pledges to the men that lie dead in France? We said that they went over there not to prove the prowess of America or her readiness for another war but to see to it that there never was such a war again. It always seems to make it difficult for me to say anything, my fellow citizens, when I think of my clients in this case. My clients are the children; my clients are the next generation. They do not know what promises and bonds I undertook when I ordered the armies of the United States to the soil of France, but I know, and

I intend to redeem my pledges to the children; they shall not be sent upon a similar errand. . . .

. . . The arrangements of this treaty are just, but they need the support of the combined power of the great nations of the world. And they will have that support. Now that the mists of this great question have cleared away, I believe that men will see the truth, eye to eye and face to face. There is one thing that the American people always rise to and extend their hand to, and that is the truth of justice and of liberty and of peace. We have accepted that truth and we are going to be led by it, and it is going to lead us, and through us the world, out into pastures of quietness and peace such as the world never dreamed of before.

After his collapse, Wilson even more adamantly opposed any concessions that would, in his opinion, impair the integrity and effectiveness of the League. Shortly before the second—and final—Senate vote on ratification, he killed any hope of compromise by directing his supporters, in this letter of March 8, 1920, to Senate Democratic leader Gilbert Hitchcock of Nebraska, to stand fast against the Lodge reservations.[12]

I understand that one or two of your colleagues do me the honor of desiring to know what my views are with reference to Article X. of the League of Nations, and the effect upon the league of the adoption of certain reservations to that article. I welcome the opportunity to throw any light I can upon a subject which has become so singularly beclouded by misapprehensions and misinterpretations of every kind.

There is no escaping the moral obligations which are expressed in positive terms in this article of the covenant. We won a moral victory over Germany, far greater even than the military victory won on the field of battle, because the opinion of the whole world swung to our support and the support of the nations associated with us in the great struggle. It did so because of our common profession

[12] *The New York Times,* March 9, 1920, pp. 1–2. © 1920 by The New York Times Company. Reprinted by permission.

and promise that we meant to establish an organization of peace, which should make it certain that the combined power of free nations would check every invasion of right, and serve to make peace and justice the more secure by affording a definite tribunal of opinion to which all must submit and by which every international readjustment that cannot be amicably agreed upon by the people directly concerned shall be sanctioned.

This promise and assurance were written into the preliminaries of the armistice and into the preliminaries of the peace itself and constitute one of the most sacred obligations ever assumed by any nation or body of nations. It is unthinkable that America should set the example of ignoring such a solemn moral engagement. . . .

I think, my dear Senator, we can dismiss from our minds the idea that it is necessary to stipulate in connection with Article X. the constitutional methods we should use in fulfilling our obligations under it. We gain nothing by such stipulations and secure nothing which is not already secured. It was understood as a matter of course at the conference in Paris that whatever obligations any Government assumed or whatever duties it understood under the treaty would of course have to be fulfilled by its usual and established constitutional methods of action. . . . .

I am sorry to say that the reservations that have come under my notice are almost without exception not interpretations of the articles to which it is proposed to attach them but in effect virtual nullifications of those articles.

Any reservation which seeks to deprive the League of Nations of the force of Article X. cuts at the heart and life of the covenant itself. Any League of Nations which does not guarantee as a matter of incontestable right the political independence and integrity of each of its members might be hardly more than a futile scrap of paper, as ineffective in operation as the agreement between Belgium and Germany which the Germans violated in 1914.

Article X. as written into the Treaty of Versailles represents the renunciation by Great Britain and Japan, which before the war had begun to find so many interests in common in the Pacific; by France, by Italy, by all the great fighting powers of the world of the old pretensions of political conquest and territorial aggrandizement. It is a new doctrine in the world's affairs and must be recognized or there is no secure basis for the peace which the whole world so longingly desires and so desperately needs.

If Article X. is not adopted and acted upon, the Governments which reject it will, I think, be guilty of bad faith to their people, whom they induced to make the infinite sacrifices of the war by the pledge that they would be fighting to redeem the world from the old order of force and aggression. They will be acting also in bad faith to the opinion of the world at large, to which they appealed for support in a concerted stand against the aggressions and pretensions of Germany.

If we were to reject Article X. or so to weaken it as to take its full force out of it, it would mark us as desiring to return to the old world of jealous rivalry and misunderstandings from which our gallant soldiers have rescued us and would leave us without any vision or new conception of justice and peace. We would have learned no lesson from the war, but gained only the regret that it had involved us in its maelstrom of suffering. If America has awakened, as the rest of the world has, to the vision of a new day in which the mistakes of the past are to be corrected, it will welcome the opportunity to share the responsibilities of Article X. . . .

The reservation proposed would perpetuate the old order. Does any one really want to see the old game played again? Can any one really venture to take part in reviving the old order? The enemies of a League of Nations have by every true instinct centered their efforts against Article X., for it is undoubtedly the foundation of the whole structure. It is the bulwark, and the only bulwark, of the rising democracy of the world against the forces of imperialism and reaction.

Either we should enter the League fearlessly, accepting the responsibility and not fearing the rôle of leadership, which we now enjoy, contributing our efforts toward establishing a just and permanent peace, or we should retire as gracefully as possible from the great concert of powers by which the world was saved. . . .

I believe that when the full significance of this great question has been generally apprehended obstacles will seem insignificant before the opportunity, a great and glorious opportunity, to contribute our overwhelming moral and material force to the establishment of an international régime in which our own ideals of justice and right may be made to prevail and the nations of the world be allowed a peaceful development under conditions of order and safety hitherto impossible.

I need not say, Senator, that I have given a great deal of thought to the whole matter of reservations proposed in connection with the ratification of the treaty and particularly that portion of the treaty which contains the covenant of the League of Nations, and I have been struck by the fact that practically every so-called reservation was in effect a rather sweeping nullification of the terms of the treaty itself.

I hear of reservationists and mild-reservationists, but I cannot understand the difference between a nullifier and a mild-nullifier. Our responsibility as a nation in this turning point of history is an overwhelming one, and if I had the opportunity, I would beg every one concerned to consider the matter in the light of what it is possible to accomplish for humanity, rather than in the light of special national interest.

If I have been truly informed concerning the desire of some of your colleagues to know my views in this matter, I would be very glad if you should show this letter to them.

WOODROW WILSON VIEWED BY HIS CONTEMPORARIES

Wilson's personality was complex and even contradictory. Although he had the ability to inspire abiding loyalties, he generated equally fervent distrusts and hatreds. His policies—domestic and even more so foreign—were as controversial as his personality. The following selections are designed not only to show the contrasting views held by Wilson's contemporaries of the man and his works, but also to provide first-hand and behind-the-scenes glimpses of his behavior at critical junctures in his career.

4

The Man

The following admiring portrait of Wilson as chief executive was written by Rear Admiral Cary T. Grayson, his personal physician, naval aide, and golfing companion.[1]

. . . Contrary to widespread opinion, he was not temperamentally cold. He was austere in his public relationships. He would not allow friendship to influence his course of duty. Several years later he told me that if he had a son who was convicted on a criminal charge, and whose case should come before him as Chief Execu-

[1] From *Woodrow Wilson: An Intimate Memoir* by Rear Admiral Cary T. Grayson (New York: Holt, Rinehart and Winston, Inc., 1960), pp. 3–7, 9, 11. Copyright © 1959 by Cary T. Grayson, Jr. Copyright © 1960 by Cary T. Grayson, Jr., Gordon Grayson, and William C. Grayson. Reprinted by permission of Holt, Rinehart and Winston, Inc.

tive, he would confirm the judgment of the court and then die of a broken heart.

Hence he was sometimes called aloof and was sometimes taxed with ingratitude. Professional politicians who placed rewards and patronage above political ethics could not understand Mr. Wilson's impersonal attitude in politics. . . .

Woodrow Wilson was never afraid of being misunderstood when a principle which he held inviolable was involved. He was not callous. He was sensitive as literary men usually are. . . .

. . . He was sincere in his principles, and he had the courage to stand for them in the face of all consequences. He broke with some of his friends, and the breaks hurt him, but these severances were due to differences on some matter of principle. He was impersonal in the sense that he would not and could not allow a friendship to stand between him and what he conceived to be his public duty.

Much has been written and will be written about his quarrels, and it has sometimes been asserted that he had no personal friends. They who say this ignore the record. For many old Princeton classmates and collegemates he kept a romantic affection to the end of his life. . . . There were associates in the Princeton faculty . . . [and] political associates, including members of his cabinet, between whom and him there was not only no break in official relationships, but an affection which endured to his life's end. . . .

By nature Mr. Wilson was kind, considerate, and extraordinarily thoughtful. . . .

His approach to most public men was courteous but not often familiar, and yet no one knew better how to lighten a serious interview with humorous repartee or anecdote. He was by nature dignified but assumed no artificial dignity. . . .

He was impatient with pompous people and intolerant of those who sought special favors from the Government. And because he cherished privacy more than display, he gave his full confidence to comparatively few, and those chiefly of his own household, of which it was my good fortune to become promptly an adopted member. . . .

He was never happier than in the bosom of his family, sitting before the fireplace in the Oval Room with us, chatting comfortably. Sometimes his conversation was playful, at other times serious. He would pun, recite nonsense verse and limericks, and then suddenly turn from merriment to gravity, frequently referring to or reading some passage from Burke or Bagehot, from which he would be likely to pass to an essay by Charles Lamb, or Birrell, or Chesterton (in whose glittering paradoxes he found expressed a good deal of his own philosophy of progressive conservatism), or to one of the poets whom he loved, Wordsworth (his favorite), or Browning (a few of whose poems he cherished deeply), or to the poetry of Matthew Arnold, for whose prose he did not care very much. . . .

Political scientist William Starr Myers, whom Wilson brought to Princeton as a preceptor, paints a far more unfavorable portrait of the man.[2]

. . . As president of Princeton Wilson showed those peculiarities of person and character which remained dominant, at least throughout all his later life, both as Governor of New Jersey and President of the United States. He was a man of strong likes and dislikes, and of dominating character. His driving force would brook no opposition. . . .

. . . Wilson was an adept in using the steamroller, and never deviated from a course he thought right, or perhaps also advantageous. On one occasion he fell into an argument with a professor of the Princeton Theological Seminary with whom he was playing a friendly game of pool. The argument became so hot that, in order to end what had become dangerous disagreement, the professor remarked, "Well, Dr. Wilson, there are two sides to every question."

"Yes," was the reply, "a right side and a wrong side!"

Furthermore, although Wilson would have been perhaps the last person to realize it, he placed everything upon a personal basis—if it were important to him. If you agreed with him you were perfect; if you disagreed, you were guilty of a personal insult. You were either his friend or his foe. He had great vision, but followed his

---

[2] William Starr Myers, "Wilson in My Diary," in William Starr Myers, ed., *Woodrow Wilson: Some Princeton Memories* (Princeton: Princeton University Press, 1946), pp. 42-44, 46. (Copyright © 1946 by Princeton University Press.) Reprinted by permission of Princeton University Press.

objectives without too great care about the possibility or the availability of the means to attain them.

There was also a strange duality of personality about the man.
In the first place, he could be as cold as a veritable iceberg when
he wanted to be. The story was told that on one occasion a student
of Princeton fell into difficulties and was about to be expelled. His
mother came to plead for him and finally was able to see President
Wilson himself, who of course seldom busied himself with the
details of such matters. Wilson was obdurate when the woman
pleaded and finally she burst into tears and said, "Dr. Wilson, if
you expel my son it will kill me!" Wilson replied, "Madam, if it is
a question between your life and the life of Princeton University,
my mind is made up."

Also he could be vindictive. During the early days in the White
House, a younger member of the faculty, as a friend of the Wilson
family, was at an informal meal with them when the conversation
turned to the subject of the late controversies at Princeton. Wilson
remarked bitterly, "I am going to expose the whole thing some
time."

In strong contrast to all this, Wilson could show a power of rare
fascination, and was then the best of companions and the most
sympathetic of friends. He had great gifts of storytelling and a
large fund of anecdotes, with a keen sense of humor, provided the
matter did not touch him personally. He would, in fact, enjoy telling jokes on himself, but never liked to have them told about him
by other people. When he was not personally concerned he could
be most generous, helpful, and nonpartisan. But if something did
affect him, he could be utterly selfish and even ruthless. . . .

Finally, it may be added that you could work *for,* but not always
with, Wilson. He would be most gracious in his directions and tell
you to "do as you think best," but there was always underneath
plainly the veiled injunction, "but do it this way." At least that is
the way I always felt. He was dominant always, or he was restless
and dissatisfied. All these things taken together may help to explain
both his great successes and his failures. He had driving power and
pushed ruthlessly ahead. . . .

> *An entry from the diary of Robert Lansing, who served as
> Wilson's Secretary of State, provides the following perceptive*

analysis of the shortcomings of Wilson's personality and mental processes.[3]

. . . When one comes to consider Mr. Wilson's mental processes, there is the feeling that intuition rather than reason played the chief part in the way, in which he reached conclusions and judgments. In fact arguments, however soundly reasoned, did not appeal to him if they were opposed to his feeling of what was the right thing to do. Even established facts were ignored if they did not fit in with this intuitive sense, this semi-divine power to select the right. Such an attitude of mind is essentially feminine. In the case of Mr. Wilson, it explains many things in his public career, which are otherwise very perplexing.

In the first place it gave a superior place to his own judgment. With him it was a matter of conviction formed without weighing evidence and without going through the process of rational deduction. His judgments were always right in his own mind, because he knew that they were right. How did he know they were right? Why he *knew* it, and that was the best reason in the world. No other was necessary. It sounds very much like the "because," which is popularly termed "a woman's reason."

In consequence to the high place, which Mr. Wilson gave to his own judgment, he was less susceptible than other men to the force of argument. When reason clashed with his intuition, reason had to give way. He was disposed to accept his sense of right rather than the result of logical deduction urged by others, no matter how expert or comprehensive their knowledge might be. Many credited this assumption of infallibility to excessive egotism, but it is more charitable and, I think, more just to charge it to his "feminist mind." Possibly the possession of such a mind constitutes a species of egotism. If it does, however, it is inherent rather than acquired. It is not the product but the producer of vanity. The common idea is that convictions reached in this way, if held by a woman, are intuitive, but, if held by a man, are evidence of egotism. I think that there may be exceptions in certain cases, which indicate that a man possesses the mentality of a woman.

[3] Robert Lansing, "The Mentality of Woodrow Wilson," diary entry of November 20, 1921, Lansing Papers (Library of Congress).

Mr. Wilson certainly disliked to deal with the details of a subject. He listened to them with impatience and sometimes with an open display of irritation. I recall that this was his attitude toward evidence of German atrocities in Belgium and toward accounts of the horrors of submarine warfare. He would not read of them and showed anger if the details were called to his attention. It is difficult to harmonize this attitude toward facts with the portrait of a sound and scientific thinker. I believe this abhorrence of being tied down to facts in forming his premises and in following the usual method of deductive reasoning, which centuries of experience had proved to be the surest and best, was because it seemed to cast doubt, as it did, on the soundness of his method.

It is of course possible that his attitude was due to an abnormal appreciation of his own mentality. In fact Mr. Wilson seemed to be constantly fearful of influences which would prevent him from forming "an independent judgment," a term which he frequently used. As a result he was constantly on his guard against advice or statements to keep this sacred "independent judgment" from the pollution of facts and the contamination of reasoned arguments. In consequence, he assumed facts, which might or might not be true, but which never were in contradiction of the decision which he had reached by intuition.

If Mr. Wilson had not been the eloquent and persuasive speaker that he was, his positive declarations of principles and policies would have been more often questioned because of the weakness of the premises on which they rested.

A man, who relies on his intuition rather than his reason, is a very poor philosopher. His philosophy is defective and cannot stand the test of critical analysis. A philosopher of this sort, if it is proper to term a person with such a mentality a philosopher, is displeased if any one points out the defects in his premises and the consequent errors in his conclusions. He seeks to avoid argument because he realizes that in a discussion of a question he lacks the knowledge of the facts to maintain his position. This inability to meet and controvert a logical argument built upon facts seemed to incense Mr. Wilson. Having convinced himself of the soundness of his own opinion, he resented any implication that his opinion might be wrong. The result was that his whole political philosophy was honeycombed with error. I have wondered if the general possession of the intuitive mind by the female sex does not account for the fact that the world has never know[n] any great women philosophers. If it does, then a man with "a feminist mind" could not be a sound philosopher.

It seems to me that this exaltation of intuition and dislike for reasoned judgments account for Mr. Wilson's antipathy for lawyers as advisers. The trouble was such advisers advanced arguments too cogent to be ignored. An intuitive decision often fared badly in their hands. This angered him as he considered their criticisms to be personal. Mr. Wilson was disposed to characterize sound and logical arguments, if opposed to his views, to be mere "technicalities," which should be brushed aside. He seemed to assume that this was the best way to treat arguments which he could not answer. If a legal adviser felt it to be his duty to persist in his opposition, he was snubbed or ignored or possibly not invited to attend further conferences on the subject under discussion.

As I see it, President Wilson's dislike for lawyers as advisers was due to the fact that they examined a matter critically and in detail. He did not seek their advice as to the soundness of his judgment, but only as to what could be urged in support of it. The consequence was Mr. Wilson avoided lawyers who did not consider him to be a sacred oracle, a fountain of absolute wisdom. As for lawyers of the other sort he had a profound contempt apparently considering them intellectually defective or dishonest. A woman might resent being asked for the reasons for her opinion, but it is hard to think of a man resenting it. Yet Mr. Wilson did resent it, particularly in the case of lawyers. This is further proof . . . that President Wilson possessed a "feminist mind."

5

Educational Reformer

Robert K. Root, whom Wilson brought to Princeton as a preceptor in English, describes the most lasting of Wilson's educational reforms—the establishment of the preceptorial system.[1]

. . . In those early years of the preceptorial system we felt that we were embarked upon a great educational adventure under the immediate guidance of a great and wise innovator. . . .

. . . Mr. Wilson described its purpose as a "bringing of undergraduates and faculty into closer and more efficient relations." That has continued to be the underlying purpose of the subsequent educational arrangements, such as the upperclass plan of study, which have further implemented Woodrow Wilson's original idea. In no other American university or college does the student have such opportunity to come into close individual relation with the mature scholars who are his teachers. He does not merely listen to lectures, however stimulating, or submit to the quizzing procedure of the class-room. In a small group of his fellows, seated about a study-table, or around an open fire, he is invited to formulate his own ideas and check their validity by the comments of fellow-students and of the older and presumably wiser student who as preceptor keeps the free discussion in paths that may lead to fruitful results.

Mr. Wilson himself described his plan as "meant to give the undergraduates their proper release from being schoolboys, to introduce them to the privileges of maturity and independence by putting them in the way of doing their own reading instead of 'getting up' lectures or 'lessons.' . . . Their exercises with their

[1] Robert K. Root, "Wilson and the Preceptors," in William Starr Myers, ed., *Woodrow Wilson: Some Princeton Memories,* pp. 15–16. (Copyright © 1946 by Princeton University Press.) All quotations from this volume are reprinted by permission of Princeton University Press.

preceptors are not to be recitations, but conferences, in which, by means of any method of report or discussion that may prove serviceable and satisfactory, the preceptors may test, guide, and stimulate their reading. The governing idea is to be that they are getting up *subjects*—getting them up with the assistance of lecturers, libraries, and a body of preceptors who are their guides, philosophers, and friends."

Some thousands of Princeton graduates of the last forty years look back to the preceptorials of their student days as the chief agent of their intellectual enfranchisement.

Mr. Wilson picked his original group of preceptors with rare skill. They came from universities all over the country. They were eager investigating scholars and devoted teachers. I think that no university in the country has ever, before or since, added to its faculty at one blow so large and so able a new recruitment. . . .

George McLean Harper, who taught French at Princeton during Wilson's presidency there, appraises Wilson's motives in putting forth his so-called quadrangle plan and the resistance the proposal aroused.[2]

. . . The administration of Dr. Patton lasted six years longer than jealous "reformers" expected; and when he retired, in 1902, Wilson was chosen president. We all hoped and expected that there would now be an increased severity in the entrance requirements and in scholastic discipline. Dr. Patton's administration had been admirable in most respects except in these matters. By appointing Professor Henry B. Fine to the deanship, Wilson made possible the raising of scholastic standards, so that Princeton became one of the hardest American colleges to enter and to remain in. Men were dropped by tens and twenties. Hard study became general. Teachers remodelled their courses and rewrote their lectures. It was a great revival. . . .

[Then] suddenly, and without sufficiently preparing the alumni,

[2] George McLean Harper, "A Happy Family," in Myers, ed., *Woodrow Wilson: Some Princeton Memories*, pp. 3–5. (Copyright © 1946 by Princeton University Press.)

trustees, faculty, and students to evaluate such a radical proposal, Wilson recommended that the institution should be reorganized for residential purposes as a group of colleges, each to consist of graduate students, undergraduates from all four classes, and several members of the faculty. Instruction, examinations, and awarding of degrees were to remain functions of the university. This is the system which has prevailed at Oxford and Cambridge for centuries, and it has great advantages: each college has its own intellectual life; the younger students get acquainted with the older ones; the fellows or residential faculty members influence the whole family. Princeton was no longer a small college where it was easy for a freshman to get acquainted with upperclassmen. It was growing rapidly, and the transmission of ideas was horizontal and no longer vertical, as it had been to some extent for three half centuries.

It was a mistake to call Wilson's proposal the "Quad Plan," for this term seemed to imply enormous expense for building new colleges. A better term would have been "collegiate system," for people would then have perceived that some, if not all, of the existing dormitories might serve as nuclei of colleges. Of course, however, the reorganization of the University would have been expensive. But a stronger source of opposition was the upperclass club system. A large amount of money and loyalty was invested in this system. Apart from the fact that it brought certain groups of juniors into daily intercourse with certain groups of seniors, it was exclusive; it was undemocratic; it was unfavorable to scholarly progress. The opposition to Wilson's plan was very strong on the part of those alumni, young, of course, who had been members of upperclass clubs. Another source of opposition was the group of loyal and generous alumni who were contributing to the establishing of the graduate college. At their head was Dean Andrew Fleming West, a man of fertile imagination and endowed with a rich gift for making friends. What would be the effect upon his great enterprise, already far advanced toward complete success, if the generosity of the alumni and other friends of Princeton were to be deflected to the broader plan? . . .

Although the trustees first approved Wilson's quadrangle plan, they reversed themselves as a result of opposition from many of the alumni and older faculty. Then followed Wilson's

*defeat in the battle over the graduate school. Edwin Grant
Conklin, whom Wilson brought to Princeton as professor of
biology, explains the issues.*[3]

. . . As the Princeton faculty was divided on the "Quad
Plan," the older members generally being against it, the younger
ones for it, so this same division of the faculty was continued in
large part in the case of the graduate college plan. The older members generally, but with some notable exceptions, lined up under
the leadership of Dean Andrew Fleming West, the younger ones
under Wilson and Dean [Henry B.] Fine. This controversy concerned primarily the *nature* of the Graduate School and only sec-
ondarily the *location* of the graduate college or residential hall.
Dean West's plans were based upon English college models and
were essentially restrictive in numbers and aristocratic socially.
Wilson and Fine on the other hand favored democratic ideals with
emphasis on productive scholarship. Of course the "outsiders" in
the faculty who had had considerable experience with graduate
work in other universities favored this latter ideal. The controversy
as to the size and location of the graduate college reflected these
two ideals; West wanted this residential hall restricted to a small
number, preferably fifty, with rather luxurious appointments, and
located at a distance from the noise and interruptions of the undergraduate campus; Wilson wanted it located in the midst of the
campus where the graduate students would infect the undergraduates with the spirit of scholarship; while Fine and the "outsiders"
insisted on provision for about two hundred graduate students in
plain but comfortable quarters. . . .

. . . I often thought that a little more spirit of compromise
might have prevented this split, but there was little if any spirit
of compromise in most of [those involved] and none at all on the
part of Wilson and Fine. . . .

But in spite of his "one-track mind" and his absolutism Woodrow Wilson was in many respects the greatest man I have ever
known. His intellectual brilliance and unexcelled ability as a

---

[3] Edwin Grant Conklin, "As a Scientist Saw Him," in Myers ed., *Woodrow
Wilson: Some Princeton Memories,* pp. 59–61. (Copyright © 1946 by Princeton
University Press.)

speaker, his breadth of vision and intense devotion to high ideals, and the real dignity of the man were evident in all circumstances. In my opinion his one chief fault was his failure to recognize the relativity of right and truth. These were absolutes with him and therefore he could not compromise with other standards and opinions. Perhaps if he had been trained in the methods and results of science, he would have realized more fully how difficult it is to avoid error and to reach perfect truth. He would have learned that man never attains to absolute truth and right but only approximates these perfect ideals, and that compromise and adjustment are the great laws of physical and social life.

6

The Conservative Hope

While at Princeton, Wilson became more and more regarded as possible presidential timber by the conservative, anti-Bryan wing of the Democratic party. In the following editorial, Walter Hines Page, the editor of the World's Work, *who was later to be one of Wilson's campaign managers in his bid for the 1912 presidential nomination and to serve as his ambassador to Great Britain, lauds his fellow transplanted southerner.*[1]

A good deal of gossip, certainly not authorized and probably irresponsible, continues to find its way into the newspapers, touching the possible entrance into high politics of President Woodrow Wilson, of Princeton University, in New Jersey. First, he was suggested as a Democratic candidate for the United States Senate, and later as a possible Presidential candidate—as an antidote proposed to the party for both Bryanism and Hearstism.

The suggestion will hardly bear fruit, it is feared; for President Wilson is not a politician, and he is a right-minded man of a safe and conservative political faith. He would not have the Government own the railroads; he would not stir up discontent; he has no fortune; he does not speak the language either of Utopia or of riot. But, if the Democratic Party should come to its senses again next year and assert its old doctrines and take on its old dignity, and seek real leadership (and pray Heaven, it may!) leaving its Bryans and its Hearsts alone, this suggestion of President Wilson is logical, sound, dignified, and decent.

Here is a man of high character, and of the best political ideals, a man who knows our history, our laws, and the genius of our people, American to the core and linked by inheritance and by train-

---

[1] *World's Work*, XII, No. 3 (January 1907), 8377.

ing to the best traditions of the past, a man who has had such executive experience as a University presidency demands (and that is a good deal), a man of a wide acquaintance, and of a mind of his own. He comes of a Southern family—was reared and chiefly educated in the South—but has lived the wider life of a citizen of the Republic. His venerated father was as staunch and beautiful a character as ever adorned and made strong the Presbyterian pulpit. Although his life has been spent in academic pursuits, he is a man of a practical mind and he knows men as well as books. He uses our language with both strength and charm; he has a sense of humour; and he is a Democrat of the best traditions. What if a political miracle should happen and the long-lost old party should find itself by nominating such a man?

7

Governor of New Jersey

*Joseph P. Tumulty, a reform-minded Jersey City
Democrat who was later Wilson's private secretary first as
governor of New Jersey and then as president, relates in his
autobiography his initial suspicions of Wilson, his transforma-
tion into a Wilson admirer, and Wilson's tactics and achievements while governor.*[1]

. . . Rumours began to circulate that the machine run by
[Bob Davis, the Democratic boss of Hudson County, ex-Senator
James Smith, Jr., and Milan Ross, Sr., of Middlesex County], the
great Democratic triumvirate of the state, was determined to
nominate the Princeton president at any cost. Young men like Mark
Sullivan, John Treacy, and myself, all of Hudson County, representing the liberal wing of our party, were bitterly opposed to this
effort. We suspected that the "Old Gang" was up to its old trick of
foisting upon the Democrats of the state a tool which they could
use for their own advantage, who, under the name of the Democratic party, would do the bidding of the corporate interests which
had, under both the "regular" organizations, Democratic and Republican, found in New Jersey their most nutritious pastures. . . .
. . . Every progressive Democrat in the Convention was opposed
to the nomination of the Princetonian, and every standpatter and
Old Guardsman was in favour of Woodrow Wilson. . . .
When the convention that nominated Woodrow Wilson had adjourned, a convention wholly dominated by reactionary bosses, it
seemed as if progress and every fine thing for which the Progressives had worked had been put finally to sleep. Behind the selection of the Princetonian and his candidacy lay the Old Guard who

[1] Joseph P. Tumulty, *Woodrow Wilson As I Know Him* (Garden City, N.Y.:
Doubleday, Page & Company, 1921), pp. 14, 17, 25–26, 31, 35, 46–51, 55, 60–61,
63, 67–68, 72–75, 77.

thought the Professor could be used as a shield for their strategy. The Progressives, both Democratic and Republican, had witnessed the scenes enacted at the Democratic Convention at Trenton with breaking hearts. . . .

The candidate soon struck his gait and astonished me and all New Jersey with the vigour, frankness, and lucidity of his speeches of exposition and appeal. No campaign in years in New Jersey had roused such universal interest. There was no mistaking the character and enthusiasm of the greeting the candidate received every place he spoke, nor the response his thrilling speeches evoked all over the state. . . .

Those of us who doubted Woodrow Wilson's sincerity and his sympathy for the great progressive measures for which we had been fighting in the New Jersey Legislature were soon put at ease by the developments of his campaign and his sympathetic attitude toward the things we had so much at heart.

No candidate for governor in New Jersey had ever made so striking and moving an appeal. Forgetting and ignoring the old slogans and shibboleths, he appealed to the hearts and consciences of the people of the state. . . .

. . . He had a theme which he wanted to expound to the people of New Jersey, which theme was the nature and character of free government, how it had been lost in New Jersey through the complicated involvements of invisible government, manipulated from behind the scenes by adroit representatives of the corporate interest working in conjunction with the old political machines; how under this clever manipulation legislators had ceased to represent the electorate and were, as he called them, only "errand boys" to do the bidding of the real rulers of New Jersey, many of whom were not even residents of the state, and how free government could be restored to New Jersey through responsible leadership. . . .

There were many surprises in the Wilson victory. The Democrats awoke on the day after the election to find that they had not only won the governorship of the state, but their joy was unbounded to find that they had captured the Lower House of the Legislature that would have the election, under the preferential primary system just adopted, of a United States senator. Therein lay the fly in the ointment.

Never in their wildest dreams or vain imaginings did the leaders of the Democratic party believe that there was the slightest chance even under the most favourable circumstances of carrying a majority of the vote of the state for the Democratic choice, James E. Martine, of Plainfield.

The suggestion that it was possible to elect a Democrat to the United States Senate was considered a form of political heresy. The nomination for the Senate had been thrown about the state until torn and tattered almost beyond repair; it was finally taken up and salvaged by that sturdy old Democrat of Union County, Jim Martine. Even I had received the offer of the senatorial toga, but the one who brought the nomination to me was rudely cast out of my office. The question was: What would be the attitude of the new Democratic leader, Woodrow Wilson, toward the preferential choice, Martine? Would the vote at the election be considered as having the full virtue and vigour of a solemn referendum or was it to be considered as Senator Smith would have it, a sort of practical joke perpetrated upon the electors? Soon the opinion of the people of the state began to express itself in no uncertain way, demanding the carrying out of the "solemn covenant" of the election, only to be answered by the challenge of Senator Smith and his friends to enter the field against Martine, the choice at the election. . . .

. . . A more politic man than Woodrow Wilson and one less sensitive to moral duty, might well have argued that this contest was the business of the Legislature, not of the Governor. Many a governor-elect would have avoided the issue on this unquestionably sound legal principle, and friends in Princeton were in fact advising Mr. Wilson to precisely this course, the course of neutrality. It would not be strange if neutrality, aloofness, had presented a rather attractive picture at times to Mr. Wilson's mind. Why should he gratuitously take a partisan position between the factions which would inevitably win for him the enmity of a strong element within the party? Which would also win for him the unpleasant reputation of ingratitude? . . .

On the other hand, there was his distinct pledge to the people during his campaign, that if they elected him governor he would make himself the leader of the party, would broadly and not with pettifogging legalism interpret his constitutional relationship to the Legislature, would undertake to assist in legislative action, and not

wait supinely for the Legislature to do something, and then sign
or veto the thing done. Moreover, he had insisted on the principle
of the preferential primary as one means by which the people
should participate in their own government and convey an expression of their will and purpose to the law-making body. The people
had voted for Martine. The fact that Senator Smith had scorned
to have his name placed on the ballot, the fact that human imagination could picture a stronger senator from New Jersey than genial
"Jim" Martine did not affect the argument. A great majority had
voted for Martine and for nobody else. Was the use of the preferential primary for the first time in the selection of a United States
senator to be ignored? . . .

It seemed as if Mr. Wilson were hesitating and holding off, reluctant to accept the gage of battle thrown down by the challenge
of the Smith wing. The leading Democratic and Independent
journals of the state were most insistent that immediate proof be
given by Governor-elect Wilson of his leadership and control over
the party and that a test should be made as to which influence,
reactionary or progressive, was to control the destinies of our party
in the state. Those of us who had followed the candidate throughout the campaign and who had been heartened by his progressive
attitude were sorely disappointed at his failure immediately to act.
It was painfully evident to us that behind the scenes at Princeton
the new governor's friends, particularly Colonel Harvey, were urging upon him cautious and well-considered action and what mayhap
might be called "a policy of watchful waiting," picturing to him
the insurmountable difficulties that would lie in his path in case he
exercised his leadership in the matter of Martine's selection to the
United States Senate. They suggested that the vote for Martine had
no binding force; that it was a mere perfunctory expression of
preference in the matter of the United States senatorship which the
Legislature was free to ignore. The only man, therefore, who could
make the vote effective was the Governor-elect himself. What he
would do in these circumstances was for days after the election a
matter of perplexing doubt to his many friends. Disappointment
and chagrin at the candidate's silence brooded over the ranks of
the progressives of the state. . . .

In his own time and by his own processes Mr. Wilson arrived at
his decision. . . . He would support Martine and use all his force,

official and personal, to have the Legislature accept the preferential primary as the people's mandate.

With prudence and caution, with a political sense that challenged the admiration of every practical politician in the state, the Princetonian began to set the stage for the preliminary test. . . .

. . . Meetings were arranged for at what were considered the strategic points in the fight: Jersey City and Newark. The announcement of the Governor-elect's acceptance of the challenge had given a thrill to the whole state and immediately the reaction against the Old Guard's attempt to discredit the primary choice was evident. The bitterness in the ranks of the contesting factions began to express itself in charges and counter-charges that were made. Speeches for and against the candidates were addressed to the ears of the unwary voter. The state was soon up in arms. There was no doubt of the attitude of the people. This was made plain in so many ways that our task was to impress this opinion upon the members of the Legislature, whose vote, in the last analysis, would be the determining factor in this contest. While we were laying down a barrage in the way of organization work and making preparations for our meetings throughout the state, the Governor-elect was conferring nightly with members of the Legislature at the University Club in New York. From day to day could be observed the rising tide in favour of our cause, and slowly its effect upon the members of the Legislature was made manifest. . . .

. . . Soon the full pressure of the opinion of the state began to be felt. Members of the Legislature from the various counties began to feel its influence upon them. Our ranks began to be strengthened by additions from the other side. The Governor's speeches and his nightly conferences were having their full effect. . . .

The State House at Trenton on the night previous to the balloting for the senatorship was a place of feverish activity. The Essex ex-Chieftain, Smith, kept "open house" in the then famous Room 100 of the Trenton House. The Governor-elect, calm and apparently undisturbed, but anxious and ready for a contest, quietly moved about the Executive offices attending to official matters.

We felt confident of the result of the vote if the members of the Legislature were left free, but we were certain that every kind of pressure would be put upon them to change the votes of the wobblers in our ranks. All night long and until four or five o'clock in the morning the Governor-elect and I remained in the Executive office, keeping in close contact with our friends both by telephone and personal conference. . . .

The election of Martine having been settled and the preferential vote having been validated through the courageous handling of a delicate situation, the new Governor was firmly in the saddle. His leadership had been tested and only the fragments of the Old Guard machine were left. The road was thus cleared of all obstacles in his own party that might be put in the way of his programme of constructive legislation.

Having delivered his first message, which contained a full and detailed discussion of his whole programme, he applied himself with great energy and industry to the task of preparing bills for introduction in the Senate and House. Not content with the mere delivery of his message, he put himself entirely at the disposal of the members of the Legislature and industriously applied himself to the task of preparation until the following measures: *Regulation of Public Utilities, Corrupt Practices Act, Direct Primaries Act,* and the *Employers' Liability Act,* were in shape to be introduced.

While his leadership was vindicated as a result of the Smith-Martine fight, the contest had undoubtedly left many bitter scars and enmities which soon manifested themselves in the unfriendly attitude of the Smith men in the Legislature toward the new Governor and particularly toward his programme of constructive legislation. For awhile after the election of Martine they seemed subdued and cheerfully resigned to defeat; but when the new Governor launched his legislative programme they began eagerly to attack it in many subtle ways. While there were some members of this group who honestly opposed the Governor's programme because of their conservative tendencies, the majority of the opposition were bent upon "putting it to sleep," because, forsooth, it bore the Wilson label. The new Governor quickly grasped the full significance of the situation and openly challenged the opposition. To accomplish his purpose, he did an unprecedented thing. He invited the Democratic members of the Legislature to meet him in the Supreme Court Room of the State House and there, face to face, he laid before them various items of his programme and challenged the opposition to lay their cards on the table. . . .

. . . This caucus gave an emphatic endorsement of his legislative programme and in a few weeks the House of Assembly had acted upon it, and the various bills that constituted his entire programme were on their way to the Republican Senate. How to induce favourable action at the hands of the Republican Senate was a problem. There were very few members of the Senate whose ideals and purposes were in agreement with those of the Governor.

When the bills reached the Senate, the Governor began daily conferences with the Republican members of that body, discussing with them the items of his programme and urging speedy action upon them. As a part of the programme of inducing the Republicans to support him, a friend of mine who was on the inside of the Republican situation reported to me that it was the opinion in the Republican ranks that the new Governor was too much a professor and doctrinaire; that he was lacking in good-fellowship and companionship; that while the members of the Legislature who had conferred with him had found him open and frank, they thought there was a coldness and an austerity about him which held the Governor aloof and prevented that intimate contact that was so necessary in working out the programme we had outlined.

We finally decided that the fault lay in the lack of social intimacy between the new Governor and the members of the Legislature. In my social and official contact with Mr. Wilson I always found him most genial and agreeable. When we were at luncheon or dinner at the old Sterling Hotel in Trenton he would never burden our little talks by any weighty discussion of important matters that were pending before him. He entirely forgot all business and gave himself over to the telling of delightful stories. How to make the real good-fellowship of the man an asset in dealing with the members of the Senate was a problem. I very frankly told him one day at luncheon that many members of both legislative bodies felt that he was too stiff and academic and that they were anxious to find out for themselves if there was a more human side to him. In order to give him an opportunity to overcome this false impression we arranged a delightful dinner at the Trenton Country Club, to which we invited both Democratic and Republican members of the Senate. The evening was a delightful one. In the corner of the little room where the dinner was served sat three darky musicians who regaled the little group with fine old southern melodies. It was real fun to watch the new Governor's conduct in this environment. He was like a boy out of school. He was no longer the college professor or the cold man of affairs. He delighted the members of the Senate who sat about him with amusing stories, witty remarks, and delightful bits of sarcasm. At the close of the dinner, Senator Frelinghuysen walked over and challenged him to a Virginia Reel. He accepted this invitation and the crowd of men were soon delighted to see the Somerset senator lead the new Governor out on the floor and his long legs were soon moving in rhythm with the music.

After all, men are just boys, and this bringing together of these practical men on so happy and free an occasion did much to convince the members of the Senate that the new Governor after all was like themselves, a plain, simple man, modestly trying to serve the interests of a great state.

This affair broke the ice, and after that there was a close intimacy between the Governor and the members of the Legislature, both Democrats and Republicans, and this coöperation soon brought about the enactment of the whole Wilson programme. Never before had so comprehensive a programme been so expeditiously acted upon by a legislative body. The Legislature had convened in January and by the middle of April every campaign pledge that the Governor had made had been kept, although the Senate with which he had to deal was largely Republican. . . .

8

Domestic Leadership

In a November, 1913 article, Saturday Evening Post
political correspondent Samuel G. Blythe appraises Wilson's
first months in the White House.[1]

The reason Woodrow Wilson dominates the members of his
party, who make up the majorities in the Senate and the House of
Representatives, is that he knows more than they do.

Occasionally, as in the present instance, an intellect is projected
into American politics—not often, but now and then. And when an
intellect is projected into American politics you observe the ordinary, standardized brand of politicians snuffling and shuffling to the
rear. We have had intellectual politicians and political intellects in
our history that operated for the broad, general good of the people
with such slants partyward as seemed desirable—and with a couple
or three angles of self-interest discernible. The difference between
those and the sort of mind that is operating just now is that the
historical ones were encumbered with fleshly—not to say fleshy—
detriments, while the Wilson dominance is a purely intellectual
proposition.

It is not my intention to assert that President Wilson has not
made mistakes—for he has—or to predict that he will not make
more mistakes. The point I want to emphasize is that the mistakes
he makes will be his own mistakes and the accomplishments will
be his own accomplishments; for, as things stand, he is the actual
Government of this country—not merely the executive head of the
nation by virtue of his presidency, but the actual Government. And
the reason for that is he knows more than the men in association

[1] Samuel G. Blythe, "Wilson in Washington," *Saturday Evening Post,*
CLXXXVI, No. 19 (November 8, 1913), 8–9.

with him. He knows he knows more, and so do they. Thus his power is complete.

Critics of the president say this undeniable strength is his chief weakness. They say he has so long been accustomed to taking a subject under consideration, thinking it out to its last details and then holding tenaciously to his conclusions, that this finality of opinion will, and has, led him into errors of performance and policy. These critics hold that he would be in better case at times if he modified his own course in accordance with the views of others fitted to advise—or, in any event, paid heed to a consensus of contrary judgment.

That criticism the president meets candidly. He often says to a protesting statesman: "I claim no superior attributes of mind or decision over you or over any man in my party; but you overlook the fact that I have been designated by the people to hold this office and be the official head of this nation. I am simply the instrument of the people for carrying out their desires as I understand them. It is my best judgment that this thing should be done in this way, and you should acquiesce in that judgment; for I must bear the burden of the responsibility to the people, and not you; and I have no desire to divide that responsibility or shift it. I have given this matter careful consideration. This procedure seems right to me. I ask you to adopt my plan. If you do not I am perfectly willing to submit both my plan and yours to the people and abide by their decision; but until the people relieve me of my responsibilities those responsibilities are paramount, and I must insist on my own conception of my duty."

There is not much of an answer for that sort of statement. The man is there, accountable, and knowing it—and accepting his trust. If the objector is not satisfied to take his opinion as final the president is satisfied to submit the matter to the people for determination; but until there is an adverse popular ruling he intends to do as he sees fit as the instrument of the people—and he does. The mistakes will be his and so will the rewards.

The majority members of the Congress of the United States having discovered how useless it is to protest, and having experienced the impersonal, logical, determined method of the man, are cowed and conquered; and, though they vigorously assert their independence among themselves, they publicly display little of it. Now and then a man rebels, but he gets nowhere. As a mass the Democrats in Congress are eager to carry out Mr. Wilson's slightest wish—eager to acquiesce in his policies and afraid to do otherwise. They are eating out of his hand. . . .

If this administration is a success it will be Wilson's success. If it is a failure it will be his failure. And the amazing thing about his complete domination is that it is not an arrogant domination, or a magisterial domination, or an offensive domination, but a suave, calm, perfectly natural result of a superior intellect dealing with inferiors. He is agreeable, mild-mannered, pleasant, even solicitous about it all; but the fact that he is affable and courteous does not alter the other fact that he is firmly and entirely the leader, and insists on complete recognition as such. He smiles when he tells a man to do a thing, but that smile does not decrease or soften the imperativeness of the order. He is a polite but not an easy boss.

The president's judgment, when once determined, may be questioned or carped at, but there is a complete understanding in Washington that it is final—I mean his judgment in large matters of policy of course. It may easily happen that he is misled on men, and it has happened. His whole method of mind during all his life has tended to make him inexpert in his assay of men; and the logic of patronage or the illogic of it is foreign to his manner of thought. So now and then the politicians, greedy for spoils, have deceived him with their candidates for office—and so, too, the necessities of partisan politics have led him to make some appointments that were not of the best. That was to be expected.

Mr. Wilson must have confidence in somebody. He has been obliged to take some men at the valuation of their sponsors, and some men have been extravagantly overvalued to him. When we reach the millennium of government all officeholders will be placed in office because of eminent fitness for their positions. Until those halcyon days arrive men will be appointed for political reasons; and political reasons will continue to be the poorest possible reasons for advent into public service.

This sort of criticism, however, is like chasing flyspecks. The main fact, as developed since March fourth last, is that, come success or come failure, this administration is Woodrow Wilson's, and none other's. He is the top, the middle and the bottom of it. There is not an atom of divided responsibility. He has accepted every issue as his, has formulated every policy as his, and is insisting—and with success —on strict adherence to his plans. The Democratic party revolves round him. He is the center of it; the biggest Democrat in the country—the leader and the chief. He will heed a protest, but considers himself under no obligation to act on it if it is not in accordance with his own conclusions. He is tenacious of his own judgments, confident of his abilities, without acting cavalierly over them—and is the president—definitely so.

According to custom the president selected a Cabinet. As a whole it is not a Cabinet to justify any loud shouts concerning its aggregate brilliance or its aggregate brain. It is a good, workaday Cabinet, with two or three high lights in it. It suits his purpose and it suits the conditions surrounding it—that Cabinet does. He wanted responsible heads for the various executive departments and he secured such heads. So far as the president is concerned his Cabinet members are just that and nothing much more—executive heads. He discusses departmental affairs with them when he discusses anything with them.

In reality Cabinet meetings on stated days have lapsed. When there is a Cabinet meeting the president sits at the head of the table and takes up with each secretary things that intimately concern him. He talks to them one at a time. While such a talk is going on the other secretaries may twiddle their thumbs or discuss the weather. They are not in it. If the president has a policy to announce or a message to read he announces the policy or reads the message to the Cabinet. He is scrupulously polite in listening to suggestions for change. He is at no pains to adopt any suggestion that does not meet with his own personal view. . . .

When President Wilson came into office there were two obvious tasks before him: The first was to revise the tariff, which has been done; the second was to revise the currency laws, which has not been done, but which is under consideration as this is written. There was no particular difficulty about the revision of the tariff. Every person in the United States who knows anything at all about the country knew the tariff must be revised. The Democrats were committed to revision. That was one of the chief factors in their success a year ago. The only question was concerning the manner and the amount of revision that were desirable.

The president had certain definite ideas on this subject. He came into office with those ideas firmly fixed. He persistently and consistently pressed those ideas. He did not move backward or forward, or up or down. He stood exactly where he stood in his tariff message and where he had stood long before he read that message. As an instance of his fixedness of purpose, let me say that last January he told me in substance what form that message would take; that it would be a tariff message, with a paragraph at the close saying that the next subject to be considered would be currency reform. And that was exactly the message he read weeks later, after all the statesmen in the Democratic party had taken a shot at advising him what to say and how to say it.

There was a good deal of backing and filling by the Democrats on the tariff. Some of them wanted this and some of them wanted that, albeit all knew they must revise it; but in the larger essentials the Democrats did what Mr. Wilson forced them to do—revised the tariff as he wanted it revised. Forced is the right word. He put on a steady pressure and never relaxed. Still the situation was made for him. They had to revise and they had to revise his way. There was no escape.

That left one of the two obvious things undone. Then came currency reform. While the Senate was making up its mind to do as the president wanted it to do about the tariff, the House passed the sort of currency bill he desired. This was easy in the House. There was some show of protest in the Democratic caucus, but the president insisted and the opposition was not effective. The House, operating under a rule, passed the Glass Bill and handed the matter over to the Senate.

Every member of the House must go before the people in 1914 for reëlection—unless he decides to quit public life. No Democratic member dared go before the people on a platform of opposition to the wishes of the president as to currency reform. They did as he said, after he had examined and revised the bill and had approved it. I am speaking now of essentials, not of minor details. He was dictator. And they were his willing subjects.

As this is written the Senate is considering the bill in committee. The Senate is a slow-moving body. There is Democratic opposition to the bill in the Committee on Banking and Currency. There will be Democratic opposition on the floor of the Senate. There is tremendous pressure from the outside.

The president is anxious to have the matter disposed of at this special session of the Congress, which must end when the regular session convenes on the first Monday in December. It is quite possible the president will not get his bill through at the special session. The subject may go over in the Senate until the regular session. There is no telling about that in these early days of October; but it is reasonably safe to say—when he does get his bill, when it finally becomes a law—he will have substantially what he wants or he will not sign the bill.

The chances are vastly in favor of the Senate's capitulating to him, rather than his giving in to the Senate. His record, method, habit of mind and practice of his prerogatives do not seem to admit of any such contingency. . . .

It is vital to the president to secure the kind of currency bill he has demanded. His chief difficulty lies in the fact that the Democrats considered the tariff a political matter—which it is, of course, under our archaic method of formulating tariffs—and nothing else. So considering it, they were susceptible to political pressure and sensitive to political obligations. They look on currency reform as a non-political question, and that is an excuse for the Senate protest—that and heavy big-business pressure. Now that is but a subterfuge; for though currency reform is non-political, of course in its basic relations to party it is as political as the tariff so far as the Democratic party is concerned, because it is a well-defined policy of this administration, and as such, from the very nature of our system, is political.

It is not likely Mr. Wilson will pay much attention to any nonpartisan spirit shown by recalcitrant senators. He wants the currency reformed and he has set forth the manner in the Glass Bill. Undoubtedly he will submit to amendments that do not annul the spirit and purpose of the Glass Bill, but he has made it a Wilson issue and will fight it out on that line. . . .

Among the most penetrating critics of the limitations of Wilson's initial reform program were the circle of progressive intellectuals associated with The New Republic. *In his book*

Drift and Mastery, *first published in 1914, Walter Lippmann
essays this devastating analysis of the New Freedom.*[2]

. . . Woodrow Wilson is an outsider capable of skilled interpretation. He is an historian, and that has helped him to know the
older tradition of America. He is a student of theory, and like most
theorists of his generation he is deeply attached to the doctrines that
swayed the world when America was founded.

But Woodrow Wilson at least knows that there is a new world.
"There is one great basic fact which underlies all the questions
that are discussed on the political platform at the present moment.
That singular fact is that nothing is done in this country as it was
done twenty years ago. We are in the presence of a new organization
of society. . . . We have changed our economic conditions, absolutely, from top to bottom; and, with our economic society, the organization of our life." You could not make a more sweeping statement of the case. The President is perfectly aware of what has happened, and he says at the very outset that "our laws still deal with
us on the basis of the old system . . . the old positive formulas do
not fit the present problems."

You wait eagerly for some new formula. The new formula is this:
"I believe the time has come when the governments of this country,
both state and national, have to set the stage, and set it very mi-
nutely and carefully, for the doing of justice to men in every relationship of life." Now that is a new formula, because it means a
willingness to use the power of government much more extensively.

But for what purpose is this power to be used? There, of course,
is the rub. It is to be used to *"restore* our politics to their full spirit-
ual vigor *again,* and our national life, whether in trade, in industry,
or in what concerns us only as families and individuals, to its purity,
its self-respect, and its *pristine* strength and freedom." The ideal is
the old ideal, the ideal of Bryan, the method is the new one of government interference.

That, I believe, is the inner contradiction of Woodrow Wilson.

[2] Walter Lippmann, *Drift and Mastery: An Attempt to Diagnose the Current
Unrest,* with introduction and notes by William Leuchtenburg (Englewood Cliffs,
N.J.: Prentice-Hall, Inc., 1961), pp. 81–85. Copyright © 1961. Reprinted by per-
mission of Prentice-Hall, Inc.

He knows that there is a new world demanding new methods, but he dreams of an older world. He is torn between the two. It is a very deep conflict in him between what he knows and what he feels.

His feeling is, as he says, for "the man on the make." "For my part, I want the pigmy to have a chance to come out. . . ." "Just let some of the youngsters I know have a chance and they'll give these gentlemen points. Lend them a little money. They can't get any now. See to it that when they have got a local market they can't be squeezed out of it." Nowhere in his speeches will you find any sense that it may be possible to organize the fundamental industries on some deliberate plan for national service. He is thinking always about somebody's chance to build up a profitable business; he likes the idea that somebody can beat somebody else, and the small business man takes on the virtues of David in a battle with Goliath.

"Have you found trusts that thought as much of their men as they did of their machinery?" he asks, forgetting that few people have ever found competitive textile mills or clothing factories that did. There isn't an evil of commercialism that Wilson isn't ready to lay at the door of the trusts. He becomes quite reckless in his denunciation of the New Devil—Monopoly—and of course, by contrast the competitive business takes on a halo of light. It is amazing how clearly he sees the evils that trusts do, how blind he is to the evils that his supporters do. You would think that the trusts were the first oppressors of labor; you would think they were the first business organization that failed to achieve the highest possible efficiency. The pretty record of competition throughout the Nineteenth Century is forgotten. Suddenly all that is a glorious past which we have lost. You would think that competitive commercialism was really a generous, chivalrous, high-minded stage of human culture.

"We design that the limitations on private enterprise shall be removed, so that the next generation of youngsters, as they come along, will not have to become protégés of benevolent trusts, but will be free to go about making their own lives what they will; so that we shall taste again the full cup, not of charity, but of liberty— the only wine that ever refreshed and renewed the spirit of a people." That cup of liberty—we may well ask him to go back to Manchester, to Paterson to-day, to the garment trades of New York, and taste it for himself.

The New Freedom means the effort of small business men and farmers to use the government against the larger collective organization of industry. Wilson's power comes from them; his feeling is with them; his thinking is for them. Never a word of understanding for the new type of administrator, the specialist, the professionally trained business man; practically no mention of the consumer—even the tariff is for the business man; no understanding of the new demands of labor, its solidarity, its aspiration for some control over the management of business; no hint that it may be necessary to organize the fundamental industries of the country on some definite plan so that our resources may be developed by scientific method instead of by men "on the make"; no friendliness for the larger, collective life upon which the world is entering, only a constant return to the commercial chances of young men trying to set up in business. That is the push and force of this New Freedom, a freedom for the little profiteer, but no freedom for the nation from the narrowness, the poor incentives, the limited vision of small competitors—no freedom from clamorous advertisement, from wasteful selling, from duplication of plants, from unnecessary enterprise, from the chaos, the welter, the strategy of industrial war.

There is no doubt, I think, that President Wilson and his party represent primarily small business in a war against the great interests. Socialists speak of his administration as a revolution within the bounds of capitalism. Wilson doesn't really fight the oppressions of property. He fights the evil done by large property-holders to small ones. The temper of his administration was revealed very clearly when the proposal was made to establish a Federal Trade Commission. It was suggested at once by leading spokesmen of the Democratic Party that corporations with a capital of less than a million dollars should be exempted from supervision. Is that because little corporations exploit labor or the consumer less? Not a bit of it. It is because little corporations are in control of the political situation.

But there are certain obstacles to the working out of the New Freedom. First of all, there was a suspicion in Wilson's mind, even during the campaign, that the tendency to large organization was too powerful to be stopped by legislation. So he left open a way of escape from the literal achievement of what the New Freedom seemed to threaten. *"I am for big business,"* he said, *"and I am against the trusts."* That is a very subtle distinction, so subtle, I suspect, that no human legislation will ever be able to make it. The distinction is this: big business is a business that has survived competition; a trust is an arrangement to do away with competition. But when competition is done away with, who is the Solomon wise enough to know whether the result was accomplished by superior efficiency or by agreement among the competitors or by both?

The big trusts have undoubtedly been built up in part by superior business ability, and by successful competition, but also by ruthless competition, by underground arrangements, by an intricate series of facts which no earthly tribunal will ever be able to disentangle. And why should it try? These great combinations are here. What interests us is not their history but their future. The point is whether you are going to split them up, and if so into how many parts. Once split, are they to be kept from coming together again? Are you determined to prevent men who could coöperate from cooperating? Wilson seems to imply that a big business which has survived competition is to be let alone, and the trusts attacked. But as there is no real way of distinguishing between them, he leaves the question just where he found it: he must choose between the large organization of business and the small.

It's here that his temperament and his prejudices clash with fact and necessity. He really would like to disintegrate large business. "Are you not eager for the time," he asks, "when your sons shall be able to look forward to becoming not employees, but heads of some small, it may be, but hopeful business . . . ?" But to what percentage of the population can he hold out that hope? How many small but hopeful steel mills, coal mines, telegraph systems, oil refineries, copper mines, can this country support? A few hundred at the outside. And for these few hundred sons whose "best energies . . . are inspired by the knowledge that they are their own masters with the paths of the world before them," we are asked to give up the hope of a sane, deliberate organization of national industry brought under democratic control.

I submit that it is an unworthy dream. I submit that the intelligent men of my generation can find a better outlet for their energies than in making themselves masters of little businesses. They have the vast opportunity of introducing order and purpose into the business world, of devising administrative methods by which the great resources of the country can be operated on some thought-out plan. They have the whole new field of industrial statesmanship before them, and those who prefer the egotism of some little business are not the ones whose ambitions we need most to cultivate. . . .

Under the pressure of winning the support of those advanced progressives who had rallied behind Theodore Roosevelt's New Nationalism in 1912, Wilson abandoned the Jeffersonian approach implicit in the New Freedom. In the following editorial, the editors of that preeminent journal of advanced liberal opinion, The New Republic, *assess Wilson's new direction.*[3]

. . . He began with a philosophical interpretation of the progressive movement which transformed it into a revival of Jeffersonian Democracy. Back of the New Freedom was the traditional Democratic confidence in free competition among individuals as the most effective means of securing the public welfare—provided only the competition was automatically regulated in the interest of fair play. The prevailing political and economic abuses were traced to pernicious Republican privileges, for which the Democrats would substitute a new Democratic Constitution of Freedom. When that new Constitution was actually framed, however, it provided rather for more government than for more freedom. The solutions were administrative rather than legal. All the Democratic legislation has depended for the accomplishment of its purposes on those expert commissions which the President had expressly disparaged during the campaign of 1912. The national banking system was finally pulled together as the consequence of autocratic powers granted to a government commission. Another commission was authorized to deal with violations of fair business practice. Finally the Democratic tariff, which is supposed to embody some approximation to freedom of trade, is found to need for its proper administration a Board of Experts. The same tendency spread by contagion to other regions of public policy. All along the line the attempt to find negative, legalistic and automatic solutions of public problems,

[3] "Woodrow Wilson," *The New Republic,* VII, No. 86 (June 24, 1916), 184–85.

with which Mr. Wilson began his presidential term, has yielded to a more active and positive attitude. . . . In Mr. Wilson's present program there is scarcely a shred left of the fabric of his Jeffersonian revival. With every development of his policy he has been approximating to the spirit and creed of a Hamilton nationalist.

Our own opinion of Mr. Wilson as a statesman has improved just in proportion as the indiscriminate and irresponsible individualism of his earlier views has yielded to a pereference for responsible nationalistic organization. He is a wiser and safer political leader today than he was four years ago—one who has a better claim on the support of intelligent liberals. . . .

9
Missionary Diplomacy

Wilson's efforts to overthrow General Huerta of Mexico brought upon him sharp attacks from two sides. On the one hand, American business interests in Mexico favored the recognition of the Huerta regime as a bulwark of order and stability. On the other, Mexicans of all shades of opinion bitterly resented Wilson's interference in their nation's affairs. Thus, even the leader of the anti-Huerta Constitutionalist movement, Venustiano Carranza, in this note to Wilson, joined in denouncing the American occupation of Veracruz in April, 1914.[1]

Pending the action of the American Senate on Your Excellency's message directed to that body, caused by the lamentable incident which occurred between the crew of a whaleboat of the cruiser *Dolphin* and the soldiers of the usurper Huerta, certain acts of hostility have been executed by the naval forces under the command of Admiral Fletcher at the port of Vera Cruz. In view of this violation of the national sovereignty, which the Constitutionalist Government did not expect from a Government which had reiterated its desire to maintain peace with the Mexican people, I comply with a duty of high patriotism in directing this note to you with a view of exhausting all honorable means before too friendly powers sever the pacific relations that still unite them.

The Mexican nation—the real people of Mexico—have not recognized as their executive a man who has sought to blemish the national integrity, drowning in blood its free institutions. Consequently the acts of the usurper Huerta and his accomplices do not signify legitimate acts of sovereignty, they do not constitute real

[1] U.S. State Department, *Papers Relating to the Foreign Relations of the United States, 1914* (Washington, D.C.: Government Printing Office, 1922), pp. 483–84.

public functions of domestic and foreign relations, and much less do they represent the sentiments of the Mexican nation, which are of confraternity towards the American people. . . .

The usurped title of "President of the Republic" cannot invest General Huerta with the right to receive a demand for reparation on the part of the Government of the United States, nor the right to grant a satisfaction if this is due.

Victoriano Huerta is a culprit amenable to the jurisdiction of the Constitutionalist Government, today the only one, in the abnormal circumstances of our nation, which represents the national sovereignty in accord with Article 128 of the Political Constitution of Mexico. The illegal acts committed by the usurper and his partisans, and those which they may yet perpetrate, be they of an international character such as those that recently occurred at the port of Tampico, or a domestic character, will be tried and punished with inflexibility and promptness by the tribunals of the Constitutionalist Government.

The individual acts of Victoriano Huerta will never be sufficient to involve the Mexican nation in a disastrous war with the United States, because there is no solidarity whatever between the so-called Government of Victoriano Huerta and the Mexican nation, for the fundamental reason that he is not the legitimate organ of our national sovereignty.

But the invasion of our territory and the stay of your forces in the port of Vera Cruz, violating the rights that constitute our existence as a free and independent sovereign entity, may indeed drag us into an unequal war, with dignity but which until today we have desired to avoid.

In the face of the real situation of Mexico—weak in comparison with the formidable power of the American nation and weaker than ever after three years of bloody strife—and considering the acts committed at Vera Cruz to be highly offensive to the dignity and independence of Mexico, contrary to your repeated declarations of not desiring to disturb the state of peace and friendship with the Mexican nation, and contrary also to the resolution of the American Senate, which has just declared that the United States does not assume any attitude inimical to the Mexican people and does not purpose to levy war against them; considering also that the hostile acts already committed exceed those required by equity to the end desired, which may be held to be satisfied; considering, furthermore, that it is not the usurper who should have the right to make reparation—I interpret the sentiment of the great majority of the Mexican people, so jealous of its rights and so respectful of the rights of foreigners, and invite you only to suspend the hostile acts already begun, to order your forces to evacuate all places that they hold in the port of Vera Cruz and to present to the Constitutionalist Government, which I as Constitutional Governor of the State of Coahuila and First Chief of the Constitutionalist Army represent, the demand on the part of the United States in regard to acts recently committed at the port of Tampico, in the security that the demand will be considered in a spirit of elevated justice and reconciliation.

Although Wilson's intervention helped bring about the overthrow of Huerta, the victorious Constitutionalists split, plunging the country into civil war. American critics of Wilson —such as Republican Senator Henry Cabot Lodge of Massachusetts, in this speech before the Senate on January 6, 1915 —blamed the administration for the resulting bloodshed and chaos and raised the demand for full-scale American military intervention.[2]

. . . President Wilson came in on the 4th of March, and on the 26th of that month the revolution headed by Carranza broke out in northern Mexico. Nothing, practically, was done in regard to Mexican affairs until the following summer, when the President sent Mr. Lind as his personal agent to Vera Cruz and subsequently delivered a message to Congress upon the Mexican situation. The instructions to Mr. Lind involved a demand in the nature of an ultimatum upon Gen. Huerta that he should abdicate. It is not usual, Mr. President, in entering into negotiations, no matter how informal or through a personal emissary, no matter how informal the emissary's position may be, to demand of the head of the Government, with whom that emissary is to communicate, that he should abdicate. Such a demand crudely stated laid us open to a telling retort, and that is the reason why the then secretary of foreign af-

[2] *Congressional Record*, 63rd Cong., 3rd sess., LII (1914–15), pt. 1, 1017–19.

fairs in Mexico was so successful in his reply. Gen. Huerta refused to abdicate. . . .

Mr. President, I was not one of those who was disposed to find fault with the refusal to recognize Gen. Huerta, although there was much to be said in favor of that course. There were broad international grounds and sound international grounds upon which that refusal could have been based. It was entirely possible to say that Gen. Huerta's government was unable to maintain international relations, for over a large area of Mexico it exercised no authority. It was possible and proper to say that the recognition might entail the validification of the loans which the Huerta government was then attempting in Europe, and which would have pledged certain revenues of Mexico, and thus deprived the United States of the opportunity of securing indemnity for injuries to its citizens.

But those grounds, Mr. President, were not put forward. The ground on which recognition of Huerta was refused was what was called a moral ground; that he was a man of bad character, who had reached the highest position in Mexico by treacherous and murderous methods. I think it highly probable that such were his methods. That is the way supreme power has generally been acquired in Mexico. It has been attained by force and accompanied by acts of violence, which are repellent to every man who believes in the reign of law and in ordered freedom.

But when we put our refusal of recognition on the personal ground that the character of the head of the Mexican Government at that time was unsatisfactory to us, to that extent we intervened. We had an absolute right on international grounds to refuse recognition, but when we say to another nation we object to the man who is at the head of your government or at the head of the only government you have got because he is a person of obnoxious character, we intervene in the affairs of that nation.

However, the refusal to recognize Gen. Huerta was based upon that ground, and while it undoubtedly embarrassed the Huerta government it did not overthrow it. He proved himself contumacious. The President, who disapproved of his methods, as we all disapproved of them, now had added to his feelings a personal resentment because Gen. Huerta had not obeyed the President's demand for his abdication. The President is a man accustomed to obedience, and I can quite understand that he should feel a natural resentment at Gen. Huerta's seeming indifference to his request.

But, Mr. President, an animosity is not a policy. The policy of the United States in regard to Mexico, speaking from the international point of view, was to secure as soon as possible the pacification of the country, the reestablishment of order, the removal of all our many causes of complaint, the security of the lives and property of our own citizens and also of the citizens or subjects of other nations, because other nations, in view of our attitude and of the Monroe Doctrine, declined to intervene and made no suggestion of intervening themselves, and that threw a moral, if not a legal, responsibility upon us. This would have been a worthy national policy, but the business of driving Huerta from power and putting somebody else in his place was not a policy at all. Nevertheless, that was the object to which our Government addressed itself. . . .

It seemed impossible to induce anyone connected with the administration to consider what was to happen after Huerta had been driven from power. When he was driven from power it became painfully obvious that no consideration whatever had been given to that point. The whole course of the administration was owing to the fact that they absolutely declined from the beginning to recognize the character of the Mexican population. It was not our business, however desirable it might be, to undertake to give Mexico new land laws or to choose a President for her. We had no protectorate over Mexico, and to regulate her internal affairs would have been intervening in the affairs of another country; but it was of the utmost importance that in our policy toward that country we should not forget of what the population consisted—50 per cent and more pure-blood Indians, some of them in a wild state; 30 per cent of half-breeds, and perhaps 20 per cent of pure Spanish blood, the descendants of the old Spanish conquerors. To suppose, with a population like that, with the history of Mexico, which apparently nobody in the administration took the trouble to read, that you could build up a government there, at a moment's notice, such as we have, let us say, in the State of Nebraska, that with those foundations you could erect an American Government on American principles, was a dream. When Huerta fell from power the result of this refusal to face facts was seen.

What has been the condition of Mexico since? As everybody who has taken the trouble to study Mexican history and to inform himself knew, the first thing was that our two allies, Villa and Carranza, fell to fighting each other. It required no great intelligence to predict that such would have been the case. . . .

As I have said, after we got Huerta out Villa and Carranza fell to fighting with each other, and look at Mexico to-day. It is a chaos of fighting factions, the prey of banditti, with predatory bands riding through the country. The social organization has collapsed, and anarchy is a polite word to apply to the condition of things.

Mr. President, I fear that it is now too late to adopt any policy which would be effective there except a complete military occupation of the country at great cost. . . .

. . . When the Mexican question was first presented to us there were but two possible policies. I am speaking now of policies and not of personal animosities. One policy was to begin by exerting all the power and influence we had under international law and under treaties and in accordance with the comity of nations to prevent outrages, to prevent wrongs, and to try to bring about pacification. This was never effectively attempted, but that is the way we should have begun, and then, in line with the policy of avoiding war at all hazards, we should have refrained from any intervention beyond the efforts warranted by international law.

The other course was to enter Mexico in sufficient force to take possession of and pacify the country and try to bring back a government there which would have the capacity of fulfilling its international obligations and at least establish order. To that course the United States was opposed, and quite naturally and rightly; but the course we did pursue was neither one or the other. It combined with singular dexterity the evils of both and the advantages of neither. We did not stay out and we did not go in effectively. . . . We have our reward for what we have done in the condition of Mexico to-day.

There was American property in Mexico to an enormous amount. I am told there was a billion dollars of American money and capital invested in Mexico—certainly many hundreds of millions. It is practically all gone. More capital, which is nothing but the savings of the American people, has been lost in Mexico in the last few years, many times over, than has been lost by the unfortunate interferences with our foreign trade which have occurred in the last few months. I was informed by gentlemen with property interests in Mexico, who came here representing many Americans employed and large American capital invested, that they were told substantially at the State Department, "We are not concerned about American property in Mexico; Americans who invest in property in foreign countries must not look to this Government to protect them." That was a new doctrine in international law to me, and I think it is a novel one to everybody. I am glad to see, Mr. President, that the indifference to American property in Mexico has not extended to American property on the high seas. I cling to the old notion that American property on the high seas and in foreign countries, when the owners of that property live in accordance with the laws of the countries in which the property is placed, is entitled to our regard and to the active protection of this Government. That protection has not been given in Mexico, and, what is far worse, between 150 and 200 American lives have been lost in Mexico. . . .

It has gone further than that. These bandits have been turned loose and have thrown themselves upon the most helpless class— upon the women, upon the priests, and upon the nuns. . . .

. . . Certainly every dictate of humanity would lead us to do what we could to save those unfortunate men and women who have been the helpless victims of these half-wild Indian soldiers. . . .

10
The Road to War

Although in practice Wilson's policies of neutrality worked in favor of the Allies and against the Central Powers, American supporters of the Allies grew increasingly impatient with and critical of his failure to take what they regarded as a sufficiently strong stand against Germany. After some initial hesitation, Theodore Roosevelt became the leading domestic champion of United States intervention on the Allied side. In the following letter of September 2, 1915, to an English friend, Arthur Hamilton Lee, the former chief executive bitterly denounces Wilson's pusillanimity toward Germany.[1]

. . . The Administration has behaved infamously. Wilson is a physically timid man. He is anxious to avoid war at all hazards. He is an entirely cold-blooded self-seeking man; and he is anxious at all hazards to keep the German-American vote and the pacificist vote. He had intended to have a neutrality which should really work in the German interest. He intended to favor Germany as much as he safely could. . . . Wilson has permitted the German Embassy to be a center of not only anti-English but of anti-American agitation, which has included the forging of passports, the purchase of newspapers, and even more sinister deeds still, for there can be little doubt that the explosions in American arms and munitions factories and on certain ships have been due to a German propaganda instigated by or connived at and encouraged by the German officials. Of course, if Wilson had any kind of self-respect, if he were a President of the Andrew Jackson or Ulysses Grant type, he would have summarily dismissed the German Ambassador and called the

[1] Excerpted by permission of the publishers from pp. 967–69 of Elting E. Morison, ed., *The Letters of Theodore Roosevelt*, Volume VIII (Cambridge, Mass.: Harvard University Press, 1954). Copyright, 1954, by the President and Fellows of Harvard College.

German Government to account for all this long ago. It has been only the successive brutalities of the Germans which have prevented him from throwing his weight on their side and against the Allies. It is only these successive brutalities which have kept American opinion aroused at all. . . .

. . . The majority of the American people . . . consists of good, decent men and women who know very little about international matters. They have no keen point of honor. They have no broad outlook. Deep in their hearts they have a high and fine purpose, which can be aroused by the right kind of appeal. But they are absorbed in their own affairs. They are horror-struck by the thought of the hideous slaughter and of all that war would bring. They do not want to face risk unless it is absolutely necessary. They do not want to leave their business or break into the easy routine of their lives if it can be avoided. Every instinct of self-interest is against their taking any action at present. They feel unwillingly and uneasily that perhaps action *is* called for. If the President told them, as Andrew Jackson or Grant, not to speak of Washington or Lincoln, would have told them, in trumpet tones, that their honor was at stake, that not only the welfare and good name of the United States but considerations of broad humanity demanded action on their part, and if he led them in such action, they would respond. But they are sincerely glad when he furnishes them with excellent excuses, excellent justifications for nonaction. He has rendered them the dreadful service of furnishing lofty names to cloak ignoble acts. These men at the outset felt stunned by the Belgium catastrophe. They felt indignation; they were uneasy lest it might be their duty to act; and they dreaded to act. If they had been told that it was their duty to act, if they had been shown that it was their duty to incur risk, if the President had led them, they would have followed. But human nature is not very strong and when these men were told by the President that it was their highest duty to be neutral not only in deed but in thought and to render the highest possible service to humanity by thus being neutral, they accepted the statement with a gasp of relief. . . .

At the same time, Wilson came under increasing attack from German-American groups for his pro-Allied, anti-German bias.

*In this open letter to the chief executive, Alphonse G. Koelble
sets forth the German-Americans' grievances.*[2]

. . . I am American born, without apologies a "German-American," which is a briefer way of identifying American citizens of German birth or descent, whose sole allegiance is to this country, and whose sentiment for the land of their fathers involves as little disloyalty to this country as does your devotion to the South, which once rebelled.

It may be that such sentiment for the land of their fathers clouds their vision in adjudging this Government's policy toward such countries, but isn't it just possible that the fact that your mother, your grandparents, and two members of your Cabinet were English born; your writings and history indicate a predilection for England, may have unconsciously biased your attitude more England way than you yourself are aware of?

Aside from that possibility, I venture to say that the record of your administration bears out the contention of the hyphenates that it has violated the spirit of neutrality, at least sufficiently to entitle them to express such opinion without being subjected to public reproval, and an attempt to set them apart from their fellows as citizens to be hazed and treated as pariahs.

And such record, incomplete: that you upheld the English contention in the Panama Canal Free Tolls question, after one President and one Congress had upheld the American contention, and by the crack of the party whip, the lure of patronage, and some "nebulous" reasons of State, you, in violation of a covenant of the party which elected you, secured the repeal of the Free Tolls Bill to the detriment of American rights and to the benefit of the English Government.

That at the very beginning of the war you censored and since have seized the German wireless and left untrammeled the English cable.

That upon its own admission your administration has allowed the English Government to "infringe upon the rights of American citizens" for a period of five months without protest;

² Alphonse G. Koelble, "An Open Letter to the President of the United States, by an American Citizen" (New York, privately printed, 1915).

That it has never specifically protested against the British declaration of the North Sea as a military area, but that only six days after Germany's declaration of the waters around Great Britain as a war zone you firmly and properly informed the German Government it would be held to strict accountability for the loss of American vessels or lives, and that in much kinder form you requested the English Government to refrain from using the American flag, although such misuse was the basis of the German declaration;

That in your first note to Germany with regard to the Lusitania, you subjected a sovereign government to a choice between war and elimination of its submarine warfare: you held Germany alone to blame for the disaster and had no word of mildest reproof for the criminal contributory negligence of the English Government in failing to protect American citizens on that ship, and in flatly rejecting after Germany accepted, this Government's proposal for removal of the causes which would have made the Lusitania disaster impossible;

That while legally the Allies are entitled to buy arms and ammunitions in the relative quantities at the opening of war, you have tolerated a shipment of arms immeasurably greater and permit this country to become in effect a base of supplies for the Allies against Germany; and while allowing such shipment which must cause the death, wounding and crippling of thousands of the kin of your fellow-American citizens, you failed to insist upon the sovereign right of this country to send food to non-combatants in Germany, thereby helping England to starve out a nation of sixty six millions of people, which has ever been friendly to us and which has contributed one-third of our population;

That at the beginning of the war you said that loans for foreign nations were "inconsistent with the true spirit of neutrality," but you have tolerated a loan of half a billion to the Allies, thereby making every investor a partisan and a potential violator of neutrality.

That you properly caused the recall of the Austrian Ambassador for interference with our domestic affairs, but British officers have been convicted of recruiting here and the British Ambassador still remains.

That you have allowed, not for a day, but for a period of eight months "an ineffective, illegal and indefensible" British blockade, which paralyzed our commerce and terminated our cotton trade, which gives employment to four millions of our people and a livelihood to many more.

That you have made unheeded protests over the flagrant British and French seizures of the Dacia, the Wilhelmina, the Greenbriar and the Hocking, and hundreds of other American vessels.

But why extend the record? The last American note to England is irrefutable corroboration of the flagrancy, the number, and the gravity of the British invasions of American rights, and your administration's total failure to stop them, and your demand to do so is in its weakness in striking contrast to your "ultimata" to Germany.

To sum up, with Germany your policy was firmness and promptness with success in every instance, to the satisfaction of Americans, while against England your policy was weakness and procrastination, and failure in every instance.

All this may be co-incidence, but it at least justifies, Mr. President, a criticism of the policy of your Government as being non-neutral, entertained not by a few, as you intimate, but by millions of your fellow citizens, hyphenates and others like myself, who are far less actuated by a sentiment for any warring nation than they are by fear and distrust of that one nation whose record of arrogance, of oppression of smaller nations, and perfidy, blackens every page of American and world history. . . .

> *Realizing that United States entry into the war would mean Germany's inevitable defeat, German Chancellor Bethmann Hollweg made repeated concessions to Wilson on the submarine issue, culminating in the so-called Sussex pledge (May 4, 1916) that submarines would not sink belligerent merchant ships without warning and without making provision for the safety of the passengers and crews. But, as he warned German Ambassador to the United States Count von Bernstoff in this telegram of May 6, 1916, the growing resentment in Germany of the American chief executive's seeming favoritism toward the Allies threatened to undermine his own position.*[3]

[3] Carnegie Endowment for International Peace, *Official German Documents Relating to the World War* (New York: Oxford University Press, 1923), II, 974–75.

We hope that our note and great concession have finally put an end to the state of distrust and have opened an era of relations of mutual confidence. Public animosity existing on this side against Wilson on account of tone and contents of his note and on account of the impression that he is taking sides against us, is in any event so marked that some action against England openly recognizable as such must be taken before he could be accepted by the German people as an unbiased person submitting his good offices in favor of peace. . . . In the absence of some such action on Wilson's part, there is danger that animosity toward him will grow and possibility of peace mediation be relegated to remotest future. Of course, in the last analysis adoption of means leading to peace is always welcome, but some action concerning England would seem necessary; in order to manifest a willingness over there to make concessions, if the peace to be brought about is not, when all is said and done, merely a peace which favors England.

If the attempt to bring England to the point of being willing to discuss the subject of peace with us, even quasi-officially, is unsuccessful, then, in view of the fact that England will probably refuse point blank to return to the Declaration of London, the great concession made by us, which commits us, to all intents and purposes, to give up U-boat warfare, will have placed us in a thoroughly untenable position. . . .

When Germany resumed its unrestricted submarine warfare, Wilson saw no alternative except to ask Congress for a declaration of war. Although an overwhelming majority of the Congress—and the country—rallied behind the chief executive, a small group of antiwar progressives voted against the war resolution. In the following speech before the Senate on April 4, 1917, George W. Norris of Nebraska blames Wilson's nonneutral policies in favor of Britain and against Germany for the crisis and accuses big business of pushing the country into the war to save their loans to the Allies and to increase the profits of the munitions makers.[4]

[4] *Congressional Record,* special session and 65th Cong., 1st sess., LV (1917), pt. 1, 212–14.

. . . The resolution now before the Senate is a declaration of war. Before taking this momentous step, and while standing on the brink of this terrible vortex, we ought to pause and calmly and judiciously consider the terrible consequences of the step we are about to take. We ought to consider likewise the route we have recently traveled and ascertain whether we have reached our present position in a way that is compatible with the neutral position which we claimed to occupy at the beginning and through the various stages of this unholy and unrighteous war.

No close student of recent history will deny that both Great Britain and Germany have, on numerous occasions since the beginning of the war, flagrantly violated in the most serious manner the rights of neutral vessels and neutral nations under existing international law as recognized up to the beginning of this war by the civilized world. . . .

The only difference is that in the case of Germany we have persisted in our protest, while in the case of England we have submitted. . . .

There are a great many American citizens who feel that we owe it as a duty to humanity to take part in this war. Many instances of cruelty and inhumanity can be found on both sides. Men are often biased in their judgment on account of their sympathy and their interests. To my mind, what we ought to have maintained from the beginning was the strictest neutrality. If we had done this I do not believe we would have been on the verge of war at the present time. We had a right as a nation, if we desired, to cease at any time to be neutral. We had a technical right to respect the English war zone and to disregard the German war zone, but we could not do that and be neutral. I have no quarrel to find with the man who does not desire our country to remain neutral. While many such people are moved by selfish motives and hopes of gain, I have no doubt but that in a great many instances, through what I believe to be a misunderstanding of the real condition, there are many honest, patriotic citizens who think we ought to engage in this war and who are behind the President in his demand that we should declare war against Germany. I think such people err in judgment and to a great extent have been misled as to the real history and the true facts by the almost unanimous demand of the great combination of wealth that has a direct financial interest in our participation in the war. We have loaned many hundreds of millions of dollars to the allies in this controversy. While such action was legal and countenanced by international law, there is no doubt in my mind but the enormous amount of money loaned to the allies in this country has been instrumental in bringing about a public sentiment in favor of our country taking a course that would make every bond worth a hundred cents on the dollar and making the payment of every debt certain and sure. Through this instrumentality and also through the instrumentality of others who have not only made millions out of the war in the manufacture of munitions, etc., and who would expect to make millions more if our country can be drawn into the catastrophe, a large number of the great newspapers and news agencies of the country have been controlled and enlisted in the greatest propaganda that the world has ever known, to manufacture sentiment in favor of war. It is now demanded that the American citizens shall be used as insurance policies to guarantee the safe delivery of munitions of war to belligerent nations. The enormous profits of munition manufacturers, stockbrokers, and bond dealers must be still further increased by our entrance into the war. This has brought us to the present moment, when Congress, urged by the President and backed by the artificial sentiment, is about to declare war and engulf our country in the greatest holocaust that the world has ever known. . . .

To whom does war bring prosperity? Not to the soldier who for the munificent compensation of $16 per month shoulders his musket and goes into the trench, there to shed his blood and to die if necessary; not to the broken-hearted widow who waits for the return of the mangled body of her husband; not to the mother who weeps at the death of her brave boy; not to the little children who shiver with cold; not to the babe who suffers from hunger; nor to the millions of mothers and daughters who carry broken hearts to their graves. War brings no prosperity to the great mass of common and patriotic citizens. It increases the cost of living of those who toil and those who already must strain every effort to keep soul and body together. War brings prosperity to the stock gambler on Wall Street—to those who are already in possession of more wealth than can be realized or enjoyed. . . .

We are taking a step to-day that is fraught with untold danger. We are going into war upon the command of gold. We are going to run the risk of sacrificing millions of our countrymen's lives in order that other countrymen may coin their lifeblood into money. And even if we do not cross the Atlantic and go into the trenches, we are going to pile up a debt that the toiling masses that shall come many generations after us will have to pay. Unborn millions will bend their backs in toil in order to pay for the terrible step we are now about to take. We are about to do the bidding of wealth's terrible mandate. By our act we will make millions of our countrymen suffer, and the consequences of it may well be that millions of our brethren must shed their lifeblood, millions of broken-hearted women must weep, millions of children must suffer with cold, and millions of babes must die from hunger, and all because we want to preserve the commercial right of American citizens to deliver munitions of war to belligerent nations.

11
The Lost Peace

Publication of the terms of the Versailles treaty brought cries of protest from many disillusioned liberals in the United States over the treaty's departures from Wilson's Fourteen Points. In this editorial of May 17, 1919, the formerly sympathetic editors of The New Republic *warn against American commitment to a League of Nations designed to uphold an unjust peace.*[1]

In the next few weeks the people of the United States must make the most important political decision that any one now living has ever been called upon to make. How it is decided and why it is decided will affect the peace and the liberty of millions. It is a decision which one may approach with unashamed solemnity for things are now at stake which go to the roots of happiness. We have to decide whether the peace which has been proposed at Paris lays the basis of an international order which has sufficient promise to justify the sacrifice of isolation. That the old isolation is in many ways no longer possible is of course obvious, but the degree in which it is to be abandoned is still a matter of deliberate judgment. In the next few weeks it is not only possible but necessary for Americans to decide just what specific obligations they will formally assume. . . .

. . . For the United States victory means neither territory, nor except in a very limited sense, reparations. It means the assumption of what at least looks like a burden, namely the use of American power to guarantee this settlement and the stability of Europe, Africa and Asia. The case for accepting this responsibility rests wholly on the assumption that by doing it the possibility of war will be greatly reduced, and the nations turned with a sense of

---

[1] "Europe Proposes," *The New Republic*, XIX, No. 237 (May 17, 1919), 67–71.

security to the enhancement of their own life. The Covenant is not
a burden if this happens, for in this larger security and social progress we should find relief from competitive armaments and a spirit-
ual enrichment by greater contact with the other nations. But if
the world as organized under the Covenant is fatally insecure, then
the obligation of trying to stabilize it in all its myriad details is indeed an entanglement and a loss of independence which it would be
wiser to avoid. . . .

. . . By the elimination of Germany and Russia and Turkey the
imperial structure of the world has narrowed at the top where it
governs and has expanded enormously at the base where it is governed. Into this new imperial system America is introduced as the
guarantor of territorial integrity against aggression, and as a voice
of protest if things go badly with the mandates. The question is of
what value that protest would be against the four Powers who actually govern the imperial system. The further question is whether
it is wise to guarantee arrangements in which the power of protest
resides in a disinterested minority of one. In other words is America
left in a position where she can affect the methods of imperialism
sufficiently to avert the disasters in which she would have to share?

The question cannot be answered offhand. For the present it is
important to note that the destruction of German imperialism
seems to carry with it not a diminution but an increase of the other
imperialisms. Even accepting the theory of the mandates at their
face value, the two great European empires—Britain and France—
and the one Asiatic empire—Japan—not only immensely increase
their absolute territory, but by the elimination of a very dangerous
competitor secure such titles as they never had before. . . .

For Germany the destruction of her overseas empire, not only
territorially but commercially is a very significant thing. It was an
easy thing for the Russian revolutionists to disdain empire. Russia is
not a modern commercial empire. But Germany is. Being an industrial nation, a large part, almost a third, of her population lives by
exchanging manufactures for food and raw materials. The existence
of markets and the assurance of materials is vital to that population,
and one of the reasons for imperialism is that it is one way, a bad
way perhaps, of recognizing this vital need and of securing the
power to enforce respect for it. If all the backward portions of the
earth were administered on strict observance of the open door and

equality of opportunity, the last vestige of excuse for imperial expansion would have disappeared. In the absence of that, a nation industrially as advanced as Germany is put indefinitely at the mercy of her business rivals if her overseas empire is destroyed. Under the treaty this absolutely essential element of recuperation is controlled for all practical purposes by Great Britain and France. One can hardly doubt that given the almost universal hatred of things German, it will be a long time before German industry can participate considerably in the world's trade.

Germany is thrown back on to her own territory, and what happens there is of the utmost importance, for sixty million people even if they are disarmed matter a great deal on a crowded continent. To Germany, destroyed as an imperial Power, the principle of nationality is applied. . . . In losing Alsace-Lorraine, part of Silesia, most of Posen, West Prussia, and the mouth of the Memel, Germany is deprived of territory which is largely non-German. The internationalization of Danzig was clearly implied in the Fourteen Points, and the districts in East Prussia, Slesvig, and at the Belgian frontier are sufficiently mixed to make a plebiscite a just and desirable solution. The Saar is another matter. There is no excuse in law or in morals for raising the question of sovereignty in the valley. It is a German valley. The armistice expressly excluded it from consideration by stating that the wrong done to France in 1871 should be righted. The Saar was not part of France in 1871, and the elaborate arrangement for the administration of the valley obviously represents a compromise between those who were and those who were not willing to act in good faith. It happens though that good faith compromised is bad faith. . . . The Saar will furnish an embittered Germany not only a real reason for discontent, but a symbol with all the necessary moral attributes, for cultivating a policy of revenge. For such a policy no reason is so good as a good reason, and in the eyes of a nation that feels itself oppressed, such a reason can easily be made the pretext for revolting against the whole settlement of the war.

The injustice will rankle and fester, and into it will be injected the poison of another injustice. Germany will point out that the principle of nationality has been applied only when it injures her and never when it might favor her. The prohibition of union with German Austria, the unconsulted annexation of the Germans in

Bohemia and the Upper Adige are of course flagrant violations of the reiterated principle of Mr. Wilson "that no right anywhere exists to hand peoples about from sovereignty to sovereignty as if they were property." Now assuming that the drastic Polish cessions are ethnically just, they are nevertheless a terrible blow to Germany because among other things they deprive her of contact with East Prussia. That they are Polish is an excellent reason for giving them to Poland, but it will not seem excellent if the principle which cuts territory away from Germany is not capable also of adding territory which is inhabited by Germans. To apply a principle one way to those "to whom we wish to be just" and refuse its application to those "to whom we do not wish to be just" is neither honorable nor good sense. In plain English it makes principles ridiculous, and having made them ridiculous to all fair-minded men among the victorious peoples, it destroys all their moral compulsion for the vanquished. The settlement can last, not because men believe in it, but because it is enforced. It is necessary therefore for Americans to consider whether they wish to guarantee the details of a settlement which could hardly have been more neatly devised to keep central Europe in an uproar.

Concealed in the question of nationality lies another, perhaps in the end, more troublesome difficulty. It happens that the territories which Germany is to lose contain a large part of her mineral wealth. . . . Lorraine iron, Saar and Silesian coal constitute three-fourths or the iron and one-third of the coal upon which German industry was based. They are gone, and the alternatives are these: either Germany secures a guaranteed supply of these minerals or a large fraction of her population must emigrate. No guarantee is contained in the treaty. With this goes the fact, discussed above, that virtually the whole apparatus of foreign trade is annihilated. It looks as if millions of Germans would have to emigrate or blow up. . . .

. . . The reparations scheme is capable of requiring Germany for a period of thirty or forty years to bear such a burden of taxation as no people has ever borne. . . .

. . . A government may sign this peace, but it will never be altogether executed. For the trouble with the treaty is that it gives the Germans too many good reasons for feeling themselves thoroughly abused. Their imperial power is destroyed, that of others is increased; the principle of nationality is worked against them; the armistice is flatly violated in the Saar; Mr. Wilson's general principles about the removal of economic barriers, no special alliances within the general family of the League of Nations, the implied promise to admit Germany to the League, all seem to have gone down the wind. With all these things done to them, it will be exceedingly difficult to keep German workingmen and Germans who were boys during the war convinced that they are suffering justly for the sins of the Hohenzollerns.

Not only will they be less and less convinced; they will be increasingly angry and vindictive. And in their anger they will have the growing sympathy of labor throughout Europe, and currents will be set up which will shake the whole edifice of European society. Looked at from the purely American point of view, on a cold calculation of probabilities, we do not see how this treaty is anything but the prelude to quarrels in a deeply divided and hideously embittered Europe.

However much the words of the Fourteen Points may be invoked to justify this treaty, one thing is so plain as to seem beyond argument. The world which will result from the document can by no stretch of language be made to agree with the picture which the President had in mind when he went to Paris, or when he spoke in the days of his glory of what was to be accomplished. His own inner disillusionment is only too apparent in the after-dinner speech which he delivered in Paris the other night. By the standards of which he himself was the most eloquent spokesman he has failed. The treaty is the work of the European governments, mitigated at a few points no doubt by Mr. Wilson. But the settlement which we are now asked to guarantee in all its detail, to underwrite with the lives and the resources of America, is one made by European governments in the spirit of the traditional diplomacy of Europe. In the meshes of that diplomacy it would be reckless folly for a nation placed as ours is to entangle itself. Therefore, assuming that the document becomes the law of Europe, the immediate task for Americans is to decide coolly just how they will limit their obligations under the Covenant. That they must be limited seems to us an inescapable conclusion.

*Although nearly all the Democrats in the Senate rallied be-
hind Wilson and the treaty, Senator Henry Cabot Lodge of
Massachusetts, the chairman of the Senate Foreign Relations
Committee, lined up most of the Republican majority in support of the following fourteen reservations to safeguard American national interests and the authority of Congress.*[2]

*Resolved (two-thirds of the Senators present concurring
therein).* That the Senate advise and consent to the ratification of
the treaty of peace with Germany concluded at Versailles on the
28th day of June, 1919, subject to the following reservations and
understandings, which are hereby made a part and condition of this
resolution of ratification, which ratification is not to take effect or
bind the United States until the said reservations and understandings adopted by the Senate have been accepted by an exchange of
notes as a part and a condition of this resolution of ratification by at
least three of the four principal allied and associated powers, to wit,
Great Britain, France, Italy, and Japan:

1. The United States so understands and construes article 1 that
in case of notice of withdrawal from the league of nations, as provided in said article, the United States shall be the sole judge as to
whether all its international obligations and all its obligations
under the said covenant have been fulfilled, and notice of withdrawal by the United States may be given by a concurrent resolution
of the Congress of the United States.

2. The United States assumes no obligation to preserve the territorial integrity or political independence of any other country or to
interfere in controversies between nations—whether members of the
league or not—under the provisions of article 10, or to employ the
military or naval forces of the United States under any article of the
treaty for any purpose, unless in any particular case the Congress,
which, under the Constitution, has the sole power to declare war
or authorize the employment of the military or naval forces of the
United States, shall by act or joint resolution so provide.

3. No mandate shall be accepted by the United States under
article 22, Part I, or any other provision of the treaty of peace with
Germany, except by action of the Congress of the United States.

[2] *Congressional Record,* 66th Cong., 1st sess., LVIII (1919), pt. 9, 8773.

4. The United States reserves to itself exclusively the right to decide what questions are within its domestic jurisdiction and declares that all domestic and political questions relating wholly or in part to its internal affairs, including immigration, labor, coastwise traffic, the tariff, commerce, the suppression of traffic in women and children and in opium and other dangerous drugs, and all other domestic questions, are solely within the jurisdiction of the United States and are not under this treaty to be submitted in any way either to arbitration or to the consideration of the council or of the assembly of the league of nations, or any agency thereof, or to the decision or recommendation of any other power.

5. The United States will not submit to arbitration or to inquiry by the assembly or by the council of the league of nations, provided for in said treaty of peace, any questions which in the judgment of the United States depend upon or relate to its long-established policy, commonly known as the Monroe doctrine; said doctrine is to be interpreted by the United States alone and is hereby declared to be wholly outside the jurisdiction of said league of nations and entirely unaffected by any provision contained in the said treaty of peace with Germany.

6. The United States withholds its assent to articles 156, 157, and 158, and reserves full liberty of action with respect to any controversy which may arise under said articles between the Republic of China and the Empire of Japan.

7. The Congress of the United States will provide by law for the appointment of the representatives of the United States in the assembly and the council of the league of nations, and may in its discretion provide for the participation of the United States in any commission, committee, tribunal, court, council, or conference, or in the selection of any members thereof and for the appointment of members of said commissions, committees, tribunals, courts, councils, or conferences, or any other representatives under the treaty of peace, or in carrying out its provisions, and until such participation and appointment have been so provided for and the powers and duties of such representatives have been defined by law, no person shall represent the United States under either said league of nations or the treaty of peace with Germany or be authorized to perform any act for or on behalf of the United States thereunder, and no citizen of the United States shall be selected or appointed as a mem-

ber of said commissions, committees, tribunals, courts, councils, or conferences except with the approval of the Senate of the United States.

8. The United States understands that the reparation commission will regulate or interfere with exports from the United States to Germany, or from Germany to the United States, only when the United States by act or joint resolution of Congress approves such regulation or interference.

9. The United States shall not be obligated to contribute to any expenses of the league of nations, or of the secretariat, or of any commission, or committee, or conference, or other agency, organized under the league of nations or under the treaty or for the purpose of carrying out the treaty provisions, unless and until an appropriation of funds available for such expenses shall have been made by the Congress of the United States.

10. If the United States shall at any time adopt any plan for the limitation of armaments proposed by the council of the league of nations under the provisions of article 8, it reserves the right to increase such armaments without the consent of the council whenever the United States is threatened with invasion or engaged in war.

11. The United States reserves the right to permit, in its discretion, the nationals of a covenant-breaking State, as defined in article 16 of the covenant of the league of nations, residing within the United States or in countries other than that violating said article 16, to continue their commercial, financial, and personal relations with the nationals of the United States.

12. Nothing in articles 296, 297, or in any of the annexes thereto or in any other article, section, or annex of the treaty of peace with Germany shall, as against citizens of the United States, be taken to mean any confirmation, ratification, or approval of any act otherwise illegal or in contravention of the rights of citizens of the United States.

13. The United States withholds its assent to Part XIII (articles 387 to 427, inclusive) unless Congress by act or Joint resolution shall hereafter make provision for representation in the organization established by said Part XIII, and in such event the participation of the United States will be governed and conditioned by the provisions of such act or joint resolution.

14. The United States assumes no obligation to be bound by any election, decision, report, or finding of the council or assembly in which any member of the league and its self-governing dominions, colonies, or parts of empire, in the aggregate have cast more than one vote, and assumes no obligation to be bound by any decision, report, or finding of the council or assembly arising out of any dispute between the United States and any member of the league if such member, or any self-governing dominion, colony, empire, or part of empire united with it politically has voted.

At the same time, a bloc of sixteen "irreconcilables" in the upper chamber—fourteen Republicans and two Democrats—insisted upon the complete and unequivocal rejection of the Covenant. In this speech delivered on November 19, 1909, just before the first vote on ratification, Republican Senator William Borah of Idaho, a leading bitter-ender, explains why he would vote against the treaty even with the Lodge reservations.[3]

. . . My objections to the league have not been met by the reservations. . . . I do not believe the reservations have met the fundamental propositions which are involved in this contest.

When the league shall have been formed, we shall be a member of what is known as the council of the league. Our accredited representative will sit in judgment with the accredited representatives of the other members of the league to pass upon the concerns not only of our country but of all Europe and all Asia and the entire world. Our accredited representatives will be members of the assembly. . . . We can not send our representatives to sit in council with the representatives of the other great nations of the world with mental reservations as to what we shall do in case their judgment shall not be satisfactory to us. If we go to the council or to the assembly with any other purpose than that of complying in good faith and in absolute integrity with all upon which the council or the assembly may pass, we shall soon return to our country with our self-respect forfeited and the public opinion of the world condemnatory. . . .

[3] *Congressional Record,* 66th Cong., 1st sess., LVIII (1919), pt. 9, 8781–84.

So, sir, we not only sit in the council and in the assembly with our accredited representatives, but bear in mind that article 11 is untouched by any reservation which has been offered here: . . . and it authorizes the league, a member of which is our representative, to deal with matters of peace and war, and the league through its council and its assembly deals with the matter, and our accredited representative joins with the others in deciding upon a certain course, which involves a question of sending troops. What will the Congress of the United States do? What right will it have left, except the bare technical right to refuse, which as a moral proposition it will not dare to exercise? . . .

Ah, but you say that there must be unanimous consent, and that there is vast protection in unanimous consent.

I do not wish to speak disparagingly; but has not every division and dismemberment of every nation which has suffered dismemberment taken place by unanimous consent for the last 300 years? Did not Prussia and Austria and Russia by unanimous consent divide Poland? Did not the United States and Great Britain and Japan and Italy and France divide China and give Shantung to Japan? Was that not a unanimous decision? Close the doors upon the diplomats of Europe, let them sit in secret, give them the material to trade on, and there always will be unanimous consent. . . .

What is the result of all this? We are in the midst of all of the affairs of Europe. We have entangled ourselves with all European concerns. We have joined in alliance with all the European nations which have thus far joined the league, and all nations which may be admitted to the league. We are sitting there dabbling in their affairs and intermeddling in their concerns. In other words, Mr. President[2]—and this comes to the question which is fundamental with me—we have forfeited and surrendered, once and for all, the great policy of "no entangling alliances" upon which the strength of this Republic has been founded for 150 years.

My friends of reservations, tell me where is the reservation in these articles which protects us against entangling alliances with Europe?

Those who are differing over reservations, tell me what one of them protects the doctrine laid down by the Father of his Country.

[2] ["Sir" and "Mr. President" here refer to the presiding officer of the Senate —Ed.]

That fundamental proposition is surrendered, and we are a part of the European turmoils and conflicts from the time we enter this league. . . .

. . . In opposing the treaty I do nothing more than decline to renounce and tear out of my life the sacred traditions which throughout 50 years have been translated into my whole intellectual and moral being. I will not, I can not, give up my belief that America must, not alone for the happiness of her own people, but for the moral guidance and greater contentment of the world, be permitted to live her own life. Next to the tie which binds a man to his God is the tie which binds a man to his country, and all schemes, all plans, however ambitious and fascinating they seem in their proposal, but which would embarrass or entangle and impede or shackle her sovereign will, which would compromise her freedom of action, I unhesitatingly put behind me. . . . .

Sir, we are told that this treaty means peace. Even so, I would not pay the price. Would you purchase peace at the cost of any part of our independence? . . . Peace upon any other basis than national independence, peace purchased at the cost of any part of our national integrity, is fit only for slaves, and even when purchased at such a price it is a delusion, for it can not last.

But your treaty does not mean peace—far, very far, from it. If we are to judge the future by the past it means war. . . .

Can you hope for peace when love of country is disregarded in your scheme, when the spirit of nationality is rejected, even scoffed at? Yet what law of that moving and mysterious force does your treaty not deny? With a ruthlessness unparalleled your treaty in a dozen instances runs counter to the divine law of nationality. Peoples who speak the same language, kneel at the same ancestral tombs, moved by the same traditions, animated by a common hope, are torn asunder, broken in pieces, divided, and parceled out to antagonistic nations. And this you call justice. This, you cry, means peace. . . . No; your treaty means injustice. It means slavery. It means war. And to all this you ask this Republic to become a party.

PART THREE

WOODROW WILSON IN HISTORY

Historical debate over Wilson and his achievements continues to rage. Controversy revolves around the man himself—the conflict between the moralist who refused to compromise with principle and the practical, even opportunistic, politician, the paradox of the nobility of his visions and the pettiness of so many of his personal relationships, the motivation for his shift to reform; over his domestic policies—the gap between his antitrust rhetoric and his policies, the limitations of his New Freedom philosophy, his attitude toward social welfare legislation; and, above all, over his foreign policies—his missionary diplomacy toward Latin America, his Far Eastern policies, his responsibility for American involvement in World War I, his role at the Paris Peace Conference and in the fight over the Treaty of Versailles, and the larger question of idealism versus realism in international affairs.

12

Hofstadter: The Conservative as Reformer

In the following selection the late Richard Hofstadter of Columbia University views Wilson as basically a conservative seeking through reform to preserve the fundamentals of the status quo.[1]

[1] Excerpts from *The American Political Tradition: and the Men Who Made It,* by Richard Hofstadter (New York: Alfred A. Knopf, Inc., 1948), pp. 236–37, 239–40, 246–49, 251–53, 255–56, 269–72. Copyright 1948 by Alfred A. Knopf, Inc. Reprinted by permission of Alfred A. Knopf, Inc., the Estate of Richard Hofstadter, and Jonathan Cape Ltd.

. . . During Woodrow's youth the Wilsons, although both were Northerners, lived at various places in the South—in Virginia, Georgia, South Carolina, North Carolina. The boy's earliest memory was of hearing that Mr. Lincoln had been elected and now there would be a war; his family lived in Augusta at the time when Sherman was ravishing Georgia. "The only place in the country, the only place in the world," said Wilson many years later, "where nothing has to be explained to me is the South." . . .

In Wilson's case it was not odd that one whose family roots in the South were so recent should assimilate himself so completely. At heart he was a sentimental traditionalist. One of the most striking things about his spirit was his urgent need to achieve a sense of belonging by affixing himself to a tradition, to a culture, to a historic body of institutions. One of his keenest limitations as an intellectual was his incapacity for detachment—not from himself, for he often held himself at arm's length, but from the political values of the society in which he lived. Neither an aggressive critic nor an intellectual innovator, he was essentially a spokesman of the past. Even as a reformer, he held up for approval not so much the novel aspects of his work as its value in sustaining the organic continuity of tradition. It was natural, then, that he should adopt wholeheartedly the traditional party of the militant South, that his first political cause should be the timeless issue of the cotton-growers—free trade.

As Wilson's political roots were Southern, his intellectual traditions were English. He liked the self-conscious traditionalism of the British thinkers. His heroes among statesmen were conservatives and Manchesterians: Burke, Gladstone, Cobden, Bright; among thinkers, Walter Bagehot, and that transplanted Englishman E. L. Godkin of the *Nation*. . . .

In his political and historical writing, Wilson was in the conventional ruling-class vein. Although he had written to John Bates Clark in 1887 that economic life should be Christianized and that "a sane well-balanced sympathizer with organized labor is very dear to my esteem," his attitude toward organized labor was generally hostile. As late as 1909 he described himself as "a fierce partizan of the Open Shop and of everything that makes for individual liberty." He had as little use for agrarian radicalism, for he was revolted by the "crude and ignorant minds" of the Populists.

As one might expect of a Manchesterian who believed that a temperate and honest pursuit of private good was a public blessing, Wilson was not nearly so critical of the business community as of Populists and trade unions. . . .

However, Wilson was far from complacent about the development of trusts. The trusts, he asserted in his *History of the American People,* gave "to a few men a control over the economic life of the country which they might abuse to the undoing of millions of men, it might even be to the permanent demoralization of society itself and of the government. . . ." But strong as his language was he seldom pursued this theme before 1912. . . .

. . . On rare occasions [while president of Princeton] he had critical things to say of entrenched wealth, particularly of bankers and speculators. . . .

But [he] . . . also made it clear again and again that he had not abandoned the conservatism of his formal political writings. He had no sympathy for Populistic democracy. Privately he proposed to knock Bryan "into a cocked hat," and publicly he remarked that the Boy Orator, though "the most charming and lovable of men personally," was "foolish and dangerous in his theoretical beliefs." He also criticized organized labor, which he called "as formidable an enemy to equality and freedom of opportunity" as the "so-called capitalistic class." Later, when he ran for the governorship of New Jersey, he was opposed by the state Federation of Labor, which could not be placated by several warm assurances that he had always criticized labor as a friend rather than an enemy.

Somehow, Wilson believed, the nation must steer a middle course between the plutocracy and the masses. The government must be an impartial agency, mediating between extremes and representing the common interest. The solution of economic problems, however, did not lie in an extreme of governmental interference or regulation. Socialism represented "a danger of the very sort we seek to escape, a danger of centralized and corruptible control." Further, it would be undesirable, even impossible, to attack all big-business combinations; those which had developed as a result of "natural forces" rather than tariff protection or unfair competitive methods were legitimate: "It is necessary to have them if modern society is to be conducted with success." To try to regulate their affairs in detail would require a series of expert commissions, and such commissions tend to go beyond regulation to the point of actually conducting business. In 1907 Wilson stated that the United States was already "on the high road to government ownership of many sorts, or to some other method of control which will in practice be as complete as actual ownership." The proper way to control business, where control was necessary, was to put good laws on the books and enforce them through the courts instead of leaving dangerously broad discretionary powers to committees. As a conservative Democrat, he said, he believed in firm and effective regulation, but repudiated "the prevailing principles of regulation, the principles which the Republican party has introduced and carried to such radical lengths. . . ." In short, he would not go so far as Theodore Roosevelt.

The solution? It must be found in a movement of moral regeneration, which would find its source in the hearts of the people and its arbiter in the government. Punishment must fall upon evil individuals—must be personal, not corporate. The corporation, he explained in one of his most frequently used metaphors, was an automobile; the maleficent corporation official was the irresponsible driver. It would be pointless to administer punishment to the machine; only innocent stockholders were penalized by fining corporations. The joyrider himself must be held responsible, and if he could not be exhorted into morality, then he must be bludgeoned. . . .

To sophisticated conservatives this approach to economic problems seemed a harmless way of draining popular discontents out of the arena of serious action. The Democratic conservatives of the North and East became interested in the political potentialities of a man who could preach such sound doctrine with so much force. . . .

It was, then, the Eastern capitalistic wing of the Democratic Party, out of the Seymour-Tilden-Cleveland tradition, within whose orbit the Wilsonian comet was first seen. . . .

. . . But no sooner had he launched his campaign [for governor] than a subtle change came over him. Forced upon the Democratic Party by the machine steamroller, his candidacy had been greeted with sharp cries of complaint by Progressives. . . . Wilson began to feel this criticism personally, and he had enough regard for the Progressives to respond to it. In a letter written toward the close of the campaign he expressed his concern "that so much credence has been given to the statement that I was out of sympathy with the point of view of the plain people, that I put conventional property rights above human rights, as it were, and held a sort of stiff academic view of things." Hitherto, in order to get a foothold in politics, it had been necessary for him to please the capitalists and the bosses; now, if he was to keep this foothold—and his own self-esteem —he must please the people. . . .

Into his speeches there crept a new and more aggressive note, a ringing demand for change, and yet for change that would preserve "established purposes and conceptions." In this idea—that we must have a forward-looking return to the past—was the link between the old and the new Wilson. . . .

In the campaign of 1912 Wilson emerged as the middle-of-the-road candidate, flanked on the right by Taft and on the left by Roosevelt in his new pose. The bulk of left-wing reform sentiment went with the Progressive Party, and many moderate Republicans seem to have deserted Taft for Wilson. Since Taft was obviously out of the running, Wilson centered his fire on Theodore Roosevelt and stressed the one issue that chiefly distinguished their points of view —the trusts. Wilson's program, the result of his first serious thinking on the trust problem, was taken from the preachings of Louis D. Brandeis and formulated with the lawyer's guidance. Wilson's speeches, the best parts of which are printed in *The New Freedom,* sound like the collective wail of the American middle class.

What has happened in America, Wilson told the voters, is that industry has ceased to be free because the laws do not prevent the strong from crushing the weak. The best, the most gifted part of the nation, the rising workingman and the thrifty ambitious bourgeois, are being cramped and confined. "The middle class is being more and more squeezed out by the processes which we have been taught to call processes of prosperity." The established interests make a concerted effort to squeeze out the beginner; they cripple his credit; they undersell him in his local market until his business withers on the vine; they discriminate against the retailer who buys from their rival; they withhold raw materials from the small man. In short, they compete unfairly.

Those who criticize the competitive order assert that free competition itself has made it possible for the big to crush the little. This Wilson denied. "I reply, it is not free competition that has done that; it is illicit competition." A big business that survives competition through intelligence, efficiency, and economics deserves to survive. But the trust is "an arrangement to get rid of competition"; it "buys efficiency out of business." "I am for big business," said Wilson, succumbing to the equivocation that invariably creeps into politicians' discussions of the trust problem, "and I am against the trusts."

The interests that have squeezed out the middle class are the same that control politics, Wilson went on. "The government of the United States at present is a foster-child of the special interests." But the people will regain control and return to their old competitive, democratic principles. "America will insist upon recovering in practice those ideals which she has always professed." The new order will be woven into the texture of the old: "If I did not believe that to be progressive was to preserve the essentials of our institutions, I for one could not be a progressive."

The New Freedom would address itself to the fundamental problem of the present age. "What this country needs above everything else is a body of laws which will look after the men who are on the make rather than the men who are already made." "The man who is on the make is the judge of what is happening in America, not the man who has made good . . . that is the man by whose judgment I, for one, wish to be guided." The hope of the nation, its real creative energies, had always been in the men "out of unknown homes" who rise to be masters of industry and politics.

Wilson conceded that there were many handsome and magnanimous reform proposals in the Progressive platform that stirred all the sympathies of a man of goodwill; but the Progressives were not even proposing to do the fundamental thing, which was to wrestle with the trusts. They proposed instead to work *through* the trusts, to guarantee, as it were, that the trusts would be merciful: "We will make these monopolies kind to you." "But," answered Wilson, "I do not want the sympathy of the trusts for the human race . . . their condescending assistance." The procedure Roosevelt stood for led up a blind alley. "You can't find your way to social reform through the forces that have made social reform necessary." The Progressive program was "perfectly agreeable to the monopolies," and for that reason "not a progressive program at all." Its method of pretended trust-control was the method proposed everywhere by "the very men who are interested in the maintenance of the present economic system of the United States." . . .

The conceptions set forth in Wilson's speeches of 1912 were translated into legislation with remarkable success and fidelity during his first four years of office. The first Wilson administration, in fact, produced more positive legislative achievements than any administration since the days of Alexander Hamilton. . . .

. . . Wilson proposed no fundamental alteration in the economic order. He still aimed to preserve competition, individualism, enterprise, opportunity—things that he regarded as vital in the American heritage. He had changed his mind, however, about regulation; his espousal of regulatory legislation by the federal government signified the abandonment of his earlier laissez-faire views. Brandeis had said during the 1912 campaign that the issue was regulated competition versus regulated monopoly, and all but the die-hards had abandoned the view that the state must keep its hands clear of the economic system. Wilson proposed that the force of the State be used to *restore* pristine American ideals, not to strike out sharply in a new direction. *("If I did not believe that to be progressive was to preserve the essentials of our institutions, I for one could not be a progressive.")* . . .

Essentially the New Freedom was an attempt of the middle class, with agrarian and labor support, to arrest the exploitation of the community, the concentration of wealth, and the growing control of politics by insiders, and to restore, as far as possible, competitive opportunities in business. . . .

But the New Freedom was forgotten during American participation in the World War, and its gains largely wiped out by the reaction that followed. Wilson's classic philosophy of competition and enterprise underwent its climactic test not in "normalcy" but in waging war and making peace. . . .

The program Wilson took to Paris envisioned a world order based upon national self-determination, free trade, and a League of Nations to keep the peace. . . . National self-determination, the international equivalent of democracy in domestic politics, would embody the principle of consent of the governed. Free trade would soften national rivalries and broaden prosperity. The League was to give security to the whole system through mutual guarantees of territorial integrity and common action against an aggressor.

Conspicuously absent from the Fourteen Points was any meaningful demand for a substantial change in international economic relations. Eight of the Fourteen Points applied the doctrine of self-determination to specific parts of Europe. The remaining six points were of general application, and of these only three dealt with economic matters: freedom of the seas in peace and in war, the removal of all economic barriers between nations, and an impartial adjustment of colonial claims. Not one of these three points represented anything more than a pious hope, and not one was even remotely realized in fact. The structure of colonial claims was hardly touched by the mandate system of the League. Freedom of the seas had to be waived at the outset upon the insistence of the British, who would not even indulge in the hypocrisy of endorsing it on principle. The removal of economic barriers was an idle suggestion if one could not remove the economic and social structures, the profit motives and systems of domestic business power that made trade barriers inevitable; Wilson dared not even try to commit his own country to further removal of trade barriers—and it was the United States that actually began international tariff warfare in the postwar era. Finally, the idea of multiplying national sovereignties and expecting a reduction of international trade barriers to follow was certainly tempting the wrath of the gods.

The peace that was signed at Versailles was a political peace in which the fundamental economic arrangements of nineteenth-century Europe were taken for granted. . . .

No wonder, then, that Wilson's League, which was not intended or designed to change the system of commercial and industrial rivalries, was inadequate to prevent war. Europe, desperately in need of economic unity under large-scale industrial technology, was partitioned into an increased number of economically unstable and strategically indefensible small states. Germany, the economic hub of the Continent, was crippled in so far as Britain and France found it in their power to do. This disorganized and broken world of competing nationalist enterprises the League was expected to preserve and make secure. The League itself did not represent a vital change, but simply an attempt to give organization to the old chaos.

No matter how historians may dramatize Wilson's struggle with Clemenceau and Lloyd George, it was not a struggle between an Old Order and a New Order, but merely a quarrel as to how the

Old Order should settle its affairs. In this attempt to organize and regulate a failing system of competitive forces the theme of Wilson's domestic leadership was repeated on a world scale. Just as the New Freedom had been, under the idealistic form of a crusade for the rights and opportunities of the small man, an effort to restore the archaic conditions of nineteenth-century competition, so the treaty and the League Covenant were an attempt, in the language of democracy, peace, and self-determination, to retain the competitive national state system of the nineteenth century without removing the admitted source of its rivalries and animosities. It had always been Wilson's aim to preserve the essentials of the *status quo* by reforming it; but failing essentially to reform, he was unable in the end to preserve. . . .

13
Blum: The Moralist in Politics

Professor John Morton Blum of Yale University assesses the sources, strengths, and limitations of Wilson's moralistic approach to politics, domestic and foreign.[1]

. . . From youth[Wilson] had determined to find principles by which men might justly order their affairs; he had wished to articulate in poetic periods his noble ideals, to identify himself with them, and to govern for them. He had for many years a calm confidence in great things to be accomplished, in his own perception through God of what they were, in his own energy and artistry to communicate them persuasively. So far as his convictions were concerned, once they were formed, discussion was adjourned. He had, he said, a one-track mind. No friend, no matter how beloved, could with impunity oppose him. Not reason, not expediency, not compassion moved him after he defined the right. . . .

Against what seemed at times to be overwhelming evidence, Woodrow Wilson sustained articles of faith common for several generations to the comfortable and polite in the United States and Europe. There was, he believed, an order in human affairs determined by God and perceivable by men. Though man was sinful and God scrupulously just, man had—he thought—a transcendent capacity to discover the rational arrangements within which his kind could wend in antiseptic harmony their several ways. This magic casement opened on a fairyland from which the perilous seas were charmed away. But like any fairyland, it needed protection from reality, from exposure to the violence and prejudice and lust that lay within the environment it was presumed to replace.

[1] John Morton Blum, *Woodrow Wilson and the Politics of Morality* (Boston: Little, Brown and Company, 1956), pp. 4, 110–111, 157–58, 197–99. Copyright, ©, 1956, by John M. Blum. Reprinted by permission of Little, Brown and Company.

Not war alone, but the impact of a multitude of personal and social problems in Wilson's time called to question his optimistic rationalism and the doctrines he derived from it. Yet consistently he maintained positions that did not satisfy the data of his senses. This was not a matter of dishonesty. He had never much relied on data. But what was more important, he fixed his own security in the doctrines he promulgated. He could not afford to modify these doctrines for fear of losing hold of his personality. He had to live in a world made up in part of his illusions. In the case of so able a man as Wilson, this led to tragedy. As he met the needs of his own personality, it also led to statements rooted in illusion, but, for that very reason, statements that transcended the apparent limits of reality, statements that composed man's most precious dreams and grandest faiths. . . .

The discharge of the duties of the Presidency created for the moralist an awkward problem. He was at once the keeper of a rigid conscience and the creature of a political system that worked only when he bent that conscience to conform to the narrow set of public tolerances. Great though it could be made, the power of his office carried him only so far; thereafter he had either to combine influence with compromise or, defending virtue, lose his way.

Something of this dilemma inhered in every executive position. Wilson at Princeton for a time made his sense of situation and persuasion the formidable implement of a serviceable ethic, but in the end obdurate certitude cost him his incisiveness and his goal. In higher office the pattern was the same. His ambitions, his obligations to his party controlled his conscious course far less than did the dictates of judicious conscience. Without offending his sensitive morality, he made his domestic reforms the expression of a common theme. Changes of mind there were, but not of heart.

So also in making foreign policy, self-searching more than self-seeking governed Wilson. His erratic course to war at every crossing took the turn marked by convictions confused but genuine. These, happily for him, impelled decisions continually acceptable to the moving national consensus. But under the best conditions this was a difficult step to keep. Wilson's was a nineteenth-century intelligence, obsolescing at a rapid rate, and this obsolescence the war accelerated. Conscience and intellect, stern, bright, intrinsically even dear, stood still while the race of time transfigured the world they understood. Fixed on its noble end, the one-track mind sensed less and less its growing isolation. . . .

. . . His basic, lifelong faith was in the individual as a distinct moral agent, inspired by and accountable to God; in the individual as the special object of a Christian education; in this individual, so accountable and so educated, as the judicious artificer of his own political and economic life. This was the essential belief of the America of Wilson's time, a belief derived from Calvin and Adam Smith and Emerson at least. It presumed, as Wilson did, that normative man was a kind of William Gladstone, that a normative nation consisted of a mass of separate human particles, each like him. But within the United States in the twentieth century, giving these particles a chance to compete was not enough; they needed also help and cohesion. Particularly in this century, moreover, liberal constitutionalism was not everywhere a possible or an attractive prospect. Some products of Wilson's faith therefore had unwholesome, unintended consequences.

The healthy heritage he left has overbalanced this. Though moralizing confuses, morals do not, nor does ascetic dedication to the task of governing. The normalcy of Warren Harding included cronyism and corruption, and a newer normalcy put influence up for hire. Wilson, in contrast, had no price. Though he trusted the invisible hand that he presumed gave guidance to men on the make, he never let these men's revelations become his scriptures. At the same time, his confidence in the individual as the proper repository of responsibility and opportunity made him suspicious alike of special privilege and of concentrated power. The former in many ways he helped to reduce. The latter he resisted rather more than the conditions of industrialism made wise, but with a spirit and in a prose that helped preserve in the United States a skepticism such as his against the day when public or private pyramids of power seemed to provide an absolute cathartic for the modern state. In office and in memory he served not just the people who elected him but also decency, the dignity of the individual, and therefore democracy.

Nor was this all. In the largest sense the end of his fight for the treaty did not come with the election of 1920. He had few friends then; indeed, men had seldom loved him. But as they ordinarily had respected him, so again they would. And in his loneliness, in his compulsion, he had always preferred their respect to their love. When he died, men wept for peace; after he died they revered again his principles; they resurrected the substance of those he held dearest —the League in the United Nations, Article X in the intervention in Korea.

Wilson's triumph was as a teacher, his lesson written in the copybooks of generations unborn when he taught. The events of a later time fastened the meaning of what he stood for in the consciousness of his successors in high office. The United States, his countrymen discovered, had to play continuously a leading part in world affairs, had to do so responsibly and morally and in company with other nations. More even than Wilson realized, discussion had to be the substitute for war. . . .

14

Link: The Higher Realism of Woodrow Wilson

*Professor Arthur S. Link of Princeton, the leading
Wilson scholar of our generation, defends Wilson, in this address at the Founders' Day celebration of the Presbyterian
Historical Society in October, 1962, against the attacks of the
so-called realist school of historians, who see Wilson as an un-
realistic visionary.*[1]

. . . The theme of this paper . . . is that among all the major statesmen and thoughtful critics of his age, President Wilson
was in fact the supreme realist, and that because this is true, what
he stood for and fought to accomplish has large meaning for our
own generation.

This is, to be sure, a very broad, perhaps even an audacious,
statement, one that does not mean very much unless we are careful
to define our terms. A realist, I take it, is one who faces life and its
situations without illusions, in short, one who can see realities or
truth through the fog of delusion that normally shrouds the earth-
bound individual. If the European and American critics of President
Wilson who thought mainly in strategic and material terms, who
measured national power by army divisions and naval bases, and
the like, if *they* were realists, then President Wilson was a realist
of a different sort. Sheerly for purposes of convenience, let us call
his view of the national and international situations with which he
had to cope a "higher realism," higher because more perceptive,
more in accord with ultimate reality, more likely to win the long-

[1] Arthur S. Link, "The Higher Realism of Woodrow Wilson," *Journal of
Presbyterian History*, XLI, No. 1 (March, 1963), 4–13. Reprinted by permission of
William B. Miller, Manager, Presbyterian Historical Society, and Arthur S. Link.

run moral approval of societies professing allegiance to the common western, humane, Christian traditions. . . .

. . . President Wilson actually had three separate public careers —as university president and educational statesman, as a domestic leader concerned almost exclusively with problems of political and economic reconstruction in the United States, and, finally, as a world statesman who attempted to give leadership in a movement for the reconstruction of the international community. He made large and seemingly different contributions in each field. And yet we must try to view his career and labors as a whole, for he was fundamentally the same man throughout. His "higher realism" was no less a force in his leadership at home than abroad.

It was evident in a striking way in the first contributions that he made as a public leader, as president of Princeton University from 1902 to 1910. There were first the things that he did and tried to do for Princeton: His introduction of a systematic and meaningful course of undergraduate study, and his positive repudiation of a chaotic free-elective system; his creation of the preceptorial, or conference, method of instruction to supplement the lecture system; and his proposal for the reorganization of undergraduate social life in order to elevate the intellectual climate of the University. By such plans and by his own inspiration, he not only transformed Princeton but also helped to transform higher education in the United States.

And yet Wilson made his greatest contributions in the field of education more by the things that he fought for than by what he did. For one thing, he stood for standards and academic integrity. For another, he had an exalted concept of the university and college and the role that they should play in preparing men and women for the nation's service because they were dedicated to the cause of truth and the intellectual enrichment of mankind. Finally, during an era of increasing specialization and degradation of undergraduate curricula by the introduction of all sorts of so-called useful programs of study, Wilson never ceased to remind fellow-teachers and administrators that their first job was to help perpetuate the cultural traditions upon which western civilization rested, not to teach students how to make money.

Who, we are entitled to ask, were the true "realists" in educational policy? Were they the alleged realists of Wilson's time, the sincere devotees of the new so-called progressive concepts and faddists, who were then beginning their long attack upon traditional studies and destroying the unity of university curricula? To ask the question is almost to answer it. The entire drive in American higher education during the past twenty years toward recovery of standards and unity in curricula and against the vulgarization that followed the widespread introduction of so-called useful courses of study—this entire movement, so full of promise, is testimony to the higher realism of Wilson's leadership in the academic world.

It was the same, I would suggest, with Wilson's leadership during his second career as Governor of New Jersey from 1911 to 1913 and President of the United States afterward. He came to political leadership at one of the most critical junctures in American history, at the high tide of what American historians call the progressive movement. For more than a quarter of a century the American people had been in revolt in city, state, and nation against corruption and venality among officeholders, irresponsibility on all levels of government, and, above all, the emergence and spread of great aggregations of economic power among railroads, banks, corporations, and so on, which were uncontrolled and often repudiated any responsibility to the people as a whole. This revolt was at the point of culmination at the very time that Wilson was catapulted into political life in 1910, and because this was true the American people were now confronted with certain choices that would determine their future political system and the role that government would hereafter play in making fundamental economic decisions.

There was, first, the choice concerning the reconstruction of the American political system. Some so-called realists of the time argued cogently from the facts that the very concept and structure of representative government were fatally defective, and that the answer lay either in direct democracy or in concentration of political power in fewer hands. "Realists" on the the other side, eager to preserve a *status quo* that benefited their own economic interests, argued just as convincingly that the American constitutional system, with its diffusion and separation of powers, was the most nearly perfect form of government on earth.

There was, secondly, the choice concerning the role that government should play in economic life. At the one extreme were the "realists" who, talking in terms of immutable economic law, defended traditional American policies of *laissez faire* in an effort to protect their privileged position. At the other extreme were "realists" with a greater popular appeal—men who demanded a sweeping extension of the power of government to bridle all hitherto uncontrolled economic interests. Some of these were socialists, ready to abandon capitalism in the major sectors of the economy altogether. Others were progressives who believed in capitalism but argued that it had reached a permanent phase of semi-monopolistic maturity in the United States and could be saved only by instituting sweeping and rigorous public controls over all important areas of national economic life.

It was Woodrow Wilson's privilege to play a decisive role in the determination of these choices. To the "realists" who had despaired of representative government in the cities and states he replied more by example than by precept—by giving a spectacular example of responsible leadership in action as Governor of New Jersey. By making representative government work on the local level he, along with a company of other leaders at the time, guaranteed its survival. To the "realists" (and he had earlier been among them) who had proclaimed the incapacity of the presidential-congressional system to cope with the great problems of national administration, Wilson responded, both by reasoned word and striking deed, by transforming that system and demonstrating that it had immensely greater capacities than the so-called realists had thought. He did this by transforming the office of President from that of an aloof presiding official into incomparably the most powerful force in the American constitutional system—the force that gave unity and direction not only to the other branches of the federal government but to public opinion as well. This, we can now see, was the "higher realism" of a man who well understood the weaknesses of the American institutional structure but who knew the fundamental strength of the American democracy far better than most so-called realists of his time.

I think that it is also fair to say that President Wilson demonstrated the same kind of long-run wisdom, or "higher realism," in leading the American people to adoption of new policies for the regulation of economic life. He rejected the arguments both of defenders of the *status quo* and of proponents of violent change as being unsound in principle and unacceptable to the majority of the people. And he (along with his supporters in Congress) instituted a series of measures to impose a large measure of public direction and control, but also to balance private initiative with public regulation in order to stimulate the enormous latent competitive energies of the people. In short, he laid the solid foundations of the present mixed American system of political economy, which, to the amazement and bafflement of many Europeans, works so curiously and so well. Viewing the subsequent development of the American economy within the framework erected by President Wilson and his colleagues, I think that we would have to conclude that Wilson's solution was the only "realistic" one that could have been adopted. It saved American capitalism by making it socially responsible and hence acceptable to the people, without, however, impeding the forces that are essential for growth in the capitalistic system.

I am sure that in talking about Wilson's "higher realism" in meeting domestic challenges, I have simply been saying things and making judgments with which virtually every historian of the United States would readily agree. It is precisely this "higher realism" that has entitled Wilson to rank, by the agreement of American historians, among the four or five most successful Presidents in our history. In talking about Wilson's policies and contributions in the realm of foreign affairs, I am, I know, on more controversial ground. Wilson was magnificently prepared for leadership in internal affairs by long study of American history and institutions. He had little if any preparation for leadership in the world at large; indeed, at the outset of his tenure in the White House he had no serious interest in foreign affairs. At the outset and later he made mistakes that still seriously impair his record. Even so, I cannot but conclude that President Wilson on the whole showed the same kind of wisdom and long-range vision and understanding, in short "higher realism," in his third career as international statesman as he had already revealed in his first two careers at home.

This, I know, is a big statement, and I would like to preface it with a few generalizations about Wilson's thought and character as a diplomat in order to lay foundations for some later observations.

The first is the most obvious and the one with which most historians would agree, namely, that President Wilson was, as I have already said, above all an idealist in the conduct of foreign affairs, one who subordinated immediate goals and material interests to what he considered to be superior ethical standards and moral purposes. His idealism was perhaps best revealed in his thinking about the purposes that the United States should serve in the world. The mission of America, he said over and over and sincerely believed, was not a mission of aggrandizement of material power but one of service to mankind. It was a mission of peace, of sacrifice, of leading the nations into a new international community organized to achieve right ends.

Secondly, all of Wilson's thinking about international relations was conditioned, in general, by a loathing for war and, in particular, by a conviction that physical force should never be used to achieve selfish and material aims.

Thirdly, Wilson was actually in many ways "realistic," even by conventional standards, in his thinking about and methods in the conduct of foreign relations. For example, he used armed force in the classic way to achieve certain diplomatic objectives in Mexico and the Caribbean. He understood the meaning of the term "balance of power." He was keenly aware of the relevance of material interests and had few illusions about the fundamental bases of international behavior. It is, one must say, the sheerest nonsense to talk about him as an impractical idealist and visionary.

Fourthly, while admitting that there were times when a nation had no recourse but to use armed force in international disputes, and while using force himself on behalf of the American government on certain occasions, President Wilson never permitted war's neuroses and fascinations either to derange his reason or to obscure the political objectives for which force was being used. Hence he was never the victim of that greatest twentieth-century delusion, that it is necessary to win wars even at the risk of losing everything for which wars are fought.

This is a very imperfect characterization of the thought and character of Wilson the diplomatist, but it may help us to understand his policies during the greatest tragedy of the modern epoch and the event that raised the gravest challenges to his leadership—the First World War. It was for Wilson a period with three distinct stages—the period of American neutrality, from August 1914 to April 1917; the period of American belligerency, from April 1917 to November 1918; and the period of peacemaking, from November 1918 to June 1919. The challenges of each period were different, but he met them all, on the whole, with the same "higher realism" that had characterized his leadership at home.

His policies during the first period can best be briefly described by saying that from the outbreak of the war in Europe to the beginning of the German unlimited submarine campaign in early 1917, President Wilson tried as hard as any man could have done to be neutral, to make the necessary accommodations to the exercise of belligerent power, and to engage in stern defense of American rights only when they could not, because fundamental human principles were involved, be compromised.

Some of the recent American "realists" have joined the older English and French critics in charging Wilson with impractical idealism precisely because he did follow such a course—because he did not rally the American people to preparation for what they have said was an inevitable participation; because he conducted long and patient negotiations to avoid a break with Germany; because he did not undertake large and early measures of assistance to the Allies and thus help to shorten the duration of Europe's agony; because he refused throughout the period of American neutrality even to align the American people and their government morally on the Allied side.

Looking back upon the final outcome, as we are entitled to do, we well might wonder who the true realists were during this period. So-called "realists," or President Wilson, who in an almost uncanny way kept himself immune from the emotional hysterias and passions that seized other men; who believed that the causes of the war were so complex and remote that it was impossible to assess the blame; who, overborne by the tragedy of the event, fought desperately to preserve American neutrality so that he could perform the healing task of reconciliation once the nations of Europe had come to some sense; who believed that an enduring peace could come only through a "peace without victory," a "peace between equals?" Who were the deluded men who had lost sight of reality? The European leaders who thought that they could win decisive victories on the battlefields and on or under the seas, and who thought that they could impose their nations' wills upon other great peoples? Or Wilson, who thought that they were momentarily mad?

The climactic confrontation, the supreme reckoning between so-called realists and the alleged impractical idealist, came once the

United States had been forced into the conflict and Germany was defeated. It did not occur earlier, because the British and French leaders had refused to permit it to occur before the Armistice was safely signed. But it could not then be long postponed, for the Allied leaders had matured their plans, and President Wilson had meanwhile formed a peace program of his own and announced it to the world in the Fourteen Points address and other speeches. . . .

The supreme task of the victors at Paris in 1919 was, obviously, to work out a peace settlement and reconstruct an international order that could endure. It had to be a peace that could survive the ebbing of passions and hatreds that consumed Europe in 1919. It had to be a peace that could survive because it could command the approval of the German people. Above all, it had to be the kind of settlement that would endure because it could retain the long-run support of the American and English peoples, even of the French people. The necessity of constructing this kind of settlement was, as we can now see clearly, the supreme reality of peacemaking in 1919. We must, therefore, judge men and measures at the Paris Conference according to whether they met this test or not.

By this criterion I do not see how any fair historian can but conclude that the so-called realists at Paris—the dedicated if cynical Clemenceau, concerned only about the destruction of the ancient foe and the future security of France; the well-intentioned Lloyd George, who had given so many hostages to war passions at home and to the Commonwealths that he was no longer a free man; and the Italians, Sonnino and Orlando, eager only for spoils—how could they be called anything other than sublime irrationalists and dreamers? Theirs was a dream, a nightmare, of unreality. Given the task of reconstructing Europe and preventing a future war, they would have responded by attempting to perpetuate the division of Europe and by making a new war almost inevitable.

On the other side and standing usually in solitary if splendid isolation was the alleged impractical idealist fighting for the only kind of a settlement that had any chance of survival—for a peace of reconciliation, for disarmament by victors as well as vanquished, against annexations and indemnities, and for a new international organization that would include former enemy states as active members from the beginning. Over and over he warned that this was the only kind of peace that would prove acceptable to the American people in the short run and to the moral opinion of the world in the long run, in short, the only kind of settlement that could endure. It should require little reference to events that followed the Paris Conference to demonstrate the "higher realism" of President Wilson's views. . . .

The result of the clash between European so-called realism and Wilsonian so-called idealism was of course the Treaty of Versailles, that compromise that violated the terms of the agreement by which the Germans had stopped fighting and made a mockery of some of the principal planks in the American President's peace program. Why, it is fair to ask, did President Wilson permit such a peace to be made and sign the treaty embodying it? The answer, I submit, is that it was "higher realism" that drove him to this difficult decision. Having won many of the things for which he had been fighting, at least partially, he had to give as well as to take, for he could not impose his will entirely upon his colleagues. He signed the Versailles Treaty in the conviction that the passage of time and the Treaty's new creation, the League of Nations, would almost certainly operate to rectify what he knew were the grievous mistakes of the Peace Conference. He signed the Versailles Treaty, in short, because he believed that it was the best settlement possible in the circumstances of 1919.

. . . The great tragedy of the postwar period was not that the Versailles Treaty was imperfect. It was that the forces of reconciliation could not operate rapidly enough without American leadership in the League, that France and Great Britain had neither the will nor the strength to defend the Treaty alone during the 1930's and, above all, that the German people submitted to demonic forces that promised a speedy rectification of all the injustices of Versailles. But this is precisely what President Wilson, in another flash of "higher realism," predicted would occur if the so-called realists, both in the United States and in Europe, continued to have their way.

That is the age-old question, whether the so-called realists or the higher realists shall have their way in determination of national and international policies. President Wilson survives a more powerful force in history than when he lived because he gave us the supreme demonstration in the twentieth century of higher realism in statesmanship.

This, obviously, was no accident. Woodrow Wilson's "higher realism" was the product of insight and wisdom informed by active Christian faith. He was not, fundamentally, a moralist, as he so often seemed to be, but a man who lived in faith, trying to be guided by the Holy Spirit in meeting the complex problems of a changing nation and world. Using one of his own metaphors we can say that the light of Heaven gleamed upon his sword. His precepts and ideals will be relevant so long as democracy endures, so long as men seek after a new international community organized for peace and the advancement of mankind.

15

Levin: Forerunner of the Cold War

In a recent provocative study, N. Gordon Levin, Jr., of Amherst College sees Wilson as the architect of an American approach to international affairs that would culminate in the present cold war.[1]

The main outlines of recent American foreign policies were shaped decisively by the ideology and the international program developed by the Wilson Administration in response to world politics in the 1917–19 period. It was these years which saw both America's entrance into World War I and the Bolshevik Revolution in Russia, the two seminal events with whose endless consequences the foreign relations of the United States have since been largely concerned. In the midst of these events, Wilsonians laid the foundations of a modern American foreign policy whose main thrust, from 1917 on, may be characterized as an effort to construct a stable world order of liberal-capitalist internationalism, at the Center of the global ideological spectrum, safe from both the threat of imperialism on the Right and the danger of revolution on the Left.

It was the Wilson Administration, in its response to the challenges of war and revolution, which forcefully articulated this conception of liberal-internationalism, a conception which had been both manifest and latent in the policies of earlier American statesmen. For Wilson, as for many of his successors in the ranks of American decision-makers, the national interest became merged with liberal ideology in such a way that he could act simultaneously as the champion of American nationalism and as the spokesman for internationalism

[1] From *Woodrow Wilson and World Politics: America's Response to War and Revolution* by N. Gordon Levin, Jr. (New York: Oxford University Press, 1968), pp. 1–2. Copyright © 1968 by Oxford University Press, Inc. Reprinted by permission.

and anti-imperialism. The policy of building a rational inter-national-capitalist order served for the Wilson Administration, at one and the same time, the varied but related tasks of countering Germany's atavistic imperialism, of answering Lenin's demands for world revolution, and, finally, of maximizing the moral and economic expansion of the liberal American nation-state. The crucial importance of Wilsonianism, then, in the context of twentieth-century American foreign relations, lies in the fact that the Wilson Administration first defined the American national interest in liberal-internationalist terms in response to war and social revolution, the two dominant political factors of our time. While many in his own generation resisted Wilson's vision of the United States as the prime mover in the creation of collective international defenses of world political and commercial order against threats from the Right and the Left, later generations of American decision-makers would seek fully to realize Wilson's design during World War II and, especially, during the Cold War that followed. . . .

Afterword

Wilson had great personal gifts. He had a keen mind, a masterful ability to appeal to the hearts and minds of his fellow men, and a personal magnetism with close friends and associates that made for abiding loyalties. But his personality had a less happy side: an inflexibility, a faith in his own rightness and righteousness, and a yearning for power that gave rise to the impression that he was a willful and arbitrary egoist.

Wilson's political philosophy was simple. He was a liberal individualist seeking to free unprivileged persons and small nations alike from the control of more powerful groups. The principles of the New Freedom and the doctrine of national self-determination both sprang from this same source. Yet this approach had grave limitations given twentieth-century realities. And even within the limits of this credo, Wilson had striking blind spots—such as regarding the Negro and civil liberties.

In the short run, Wilson the domestic reformer was highly successful. But the inherent limitations of his progressivism—aggravated by his growing preoccupation with foreign affairs—left him unprepared to deal with the grave problems that the United States faced in the aftermath of World War I.

His worst shortcomings were revealed in the realm of foreign affairs. Wilson was not devoid of appreciation of the role of economic forces in international affairs, nor was he blind to the importance of the national interest and national security. Yet his fundamentally moralistic approach to foreign problems led him into a series of contradictions—Wilson, the antiimperialist, becoming entangled in a brand of moral imperialism as obnoxious to its supposed beneficiaries as the "dollar diplomacy" he so loudly foreswore; Wilson, the lover of peace, leading the United States into the bloody morass of World War I; Wilson, the apostle of American participation in a system of collective security, not only destroying by his own inflexibility his dream of American membership in the League of Nations, but, by overselling the purposes of American involvement and raising inflated hopes about the future, contributing to the popular disillusionment that so handicapped this country's response to the threat of aggression in the 1930s.

Above all, Wilson's rejection of the traditional view of America as standing aloof from the rest of the world as the city upon the hill would have dubious long-range consequences. The positive side, the dream of an association of nations to limit the destructive effects of unrestrained national sovereignty, continues to exert a powerful appeal upon the popular imagination. But its embodiment, first in the League of Nations and then in the United Nations, has foundered upon the shoals of intractable national power rivalries. And its less happy aspect, its vision of the United States as the policeman of the world, has culminated in this country's involvement in an increasingly unpopular war far distant from its shores.

WILSON AND THE HISTORIANS

It has become a truism that historical objectivity will forever remain, in Charles Beard's words, "that noble dream." So not surprisingly, Wilson's historical image has undergone marked changes over time. In part, this has been the result of the opening of previously untapped sources. But even more important have been the changes that have taken place in the general climate of opinion.

Although there remained a band of dedicated Wilsonians who continued to hold aloft his banner, the bulk of the writing on Wilson during the 1920s and 1930s tended to be critical. The mood of the era of normalcy was inhospitable to reform, and even after the depression many of the new generation of reformers found little of relevance in the Wilsonian heritage. Above all, disillusionment with American involvement in World War I and with the workings of the League of Nations combined with fears of this country's involvement in a second conflagration to spur bitter attacks upon Wilson's foreign policies.

In the aftermath of World War II, reform-minded historians seeking to legitimize New Deal and post–New Deal developments by postulating a continuing American reform tradition restored Wilson to the pantheon of domestic heroes. At the same time, historians tended—largely unconsciously—to equate Hitler's Germany with Imperial Germany and thus to look more favorably upon American involvement in World War I. Furthermore, the postwar commitment to collective security through the United Nations brought renewed popularity to Wilson as the champion of the ideal of a world organization.

But the cold war has stimulated a reaction. On the one hand, the advocates of greater realism in American foreign policy reject Wilson's moralism and assail him for ignoring power realities. On the other hand, writers of the New Left persuasion deplore Wilson's antirevolutionary bias and see in his commitment to preserving a liberal-capitalist internationalism the roots of the confrontation with the Soviet Union.

Despite this reaction, Wilson's current reputation among historians remains high. Polls of historians conducted by Arthur M. Schlesinger in 1948 and 1952 ranked Wilson among the "great" presidents, fourth behind Lincoln, Washington, and Franklin D. Roosevelt. A more methodologically sophisticated poll of historians published in 1970 showed a more mixed, but still highly favorable, response. Although Wilson was rated lowest among all presidents in the flexibility of his approach in implementing his programs and policies, he was rated first, and by a wide margin, in his idealism; fifth (behind FDR, Lincoln, Jackson, and TR) in the strength of his role in directing the government and shaping the events of his day; seventh (behind FDR, TR, Jackson, Lyndon Johnson, Truman, and Kennedy) in his presidential activism; seventh (behind Lincoln, FDR, Washington, Jefferson, TR, and Truman) in the significance of his accomplishments as president; and sixth (behind Lincoln, Washington, FDR, Jefferson, and TR) in his general prestige at the time of the poll.[1]

[1] Gary M. Maranell, "The Evaluation of Presidents: An Extension of the Schlesinger Polls," *Journal of American History*, LVII (1970), 104–13.

Bibliographical Note

The published literature on Woodrow Wilson is voluminous and growing with each passing year. There is no comprehensive up-to-date bibliography. Arthur S. Link and William Leary, Jr., *The Progressive Era and the Great War, 1896–1920* (New York, 1969), is a useful listing of books and articles. But students should also consult the following more interpretive bibliographical essays: Richard W. Leopold, "The Problem of American Intervention in 1917: An Historical Retrospect," *World Politics,* II (1950), 404–25; Richard L. Watson, Jr., "Woodrow Wilson and His Interpreters, 1947–1957," *Mississippi Valley Historical Review,* XLIV (1957); 207–36; George E. Mowry, *The Progressive Movement, 1900–1920: Recent Ideas and New Literature* (Washington, D.C., 1958); and Ernest R. May, *American Intervention: 1917 and 1941* (Washington, D.C., 1960).

Laura S. Turnbull, *Woodrow Wilson: A Selected Bibliography of His Published Writings, Addresses, and Public Papers* (Princeton, 1948), is a helpful guide to published materials by Wilson himself. The fullest available collection of Wilson source material is Ray Stannard Baker and William E. Dodd, eds., *The Public Papers of Woodrow Wilson,* 6 vols. (New York, 1925–27). This work is in the process of being superseded by Arthur S. Link et al., eds., *The Papers of Woodrow Wilson,* 11 vols. to date (Princeton, 1966–   ); but Vol. XI goes up only to 1900. David W. Hirst, *Woodrow Wilson, Reform Governor: A Documentary Narrative* (Princeton, 1965), is an invaluable compilation for his term as governor of New Jersey. William Bayard Hale edited some of Wilson's 1912 campaign speeches under the title Woodrow Wilson, *The New Freedom: A Call for the Emancipation of the Generous Energies of a People* (New York, 1913); a more comprehensive and complete collection of these speeches is John Wells Davidson, ed., *A Crossroads of Freedom: The 1912 Campaign Speeches of Woodrow Wilson* (New Haven, 1956). Selections from Wilson's public and private writings are reprinted in Donald Day, ed., *Woodrow Wilson's Own Story* (Boston, 1952); August Heckscher, ed., *The Politics of Woodrow Wilson:*

Selections from His Speeches and Writings (New York, 1956); and E. David Cronon, ed., *The Political Thought of Woodrow Wilson* (Indianapolis, 1965).

Memoirs and the published diaries and letters of contemporaries and associates constitute an important source of information about Wilson. Eleanor Wilson McAdoo, *The Woodrow Wilsons* (New York, 1937), and Margaret Randolph Elliott, *My Aunt Louisa and Woodrow Wilson* (Chapel Hill, N.C., 1944), shed light upon his family life. His daughter Eleanor Wilson McAdoo edited his correspondence with his first wife: *The Priceless Gift: The Love Letters of Woodrow Wilson and Ellen Axson Wilson* (New York, 1962). William Starr Myers, ed., *Woodrow Wilson: Some Princeton Memories* (Princeton, 1946), contains recollections of Princeton contemporaries. Joseph P. Tumulty, *Woodrow Wilson As I Know Him* (Garden City, N.Y., 1921), and James Kerney, *The Political Education of Woodrow Wilson* (New York, 1926), are particularly valuable for the gubernatorial years. Tumulty was personally closer to Wilson; Kerney is more detached and penetrating. William F. McCombs's account of the 1912 presidential nomination and campaign, *Making Woodrow Wilson President* (New York, 1921), is colored by his subsequent bitterness toward Wilson. The extracts from the House diaries and from House's letters to Wilson in Charles Seymour, ed., *The Intimate Papers of Colonel House,* 4 vols. (Boston, 1926–28), make these volumes a major source for the presidential years. Edith Bolling Wilson's *My Memoir* (Indianapolis, 1939) and the account by Wilson's personal physician, Cary T. Grayson, *Woodrow Wilson: An Intimate Memoir* (New York, 1960), are indispensable for Wilson's illness and last years.

Most of the members of Wilson's official family while he was president published their reminiscences: all three of his secretaries of state, *The Memoirs of William Jennings Bryan,* ed. Mary B. Bryan (Philadelphia, 1925); Robert Lansing, *The Big Four and Others of the Peace Conference* (Boston, 1921), *The Peace Negotiations: A Personal Narrative* (Boston, 1921), and *War Memoirs of Robert Lansing* (Indianapolis, 1935); and Bainbridge Colby, *The Close of Woodrow Wilson's Administration and the Final Years* (New York, 1930); Vice-President Thomas R. Marshall, *Recollections of Thomas R. Marshall* (Indianapolis, 1925); Secretary of Agriculture David F. Houston, *Eight Years with Wilson's Cabinet, 1913–1920,* 2 vols.

(Garden City, N.Y., 1926); Secretary of Commerce William C. Redfield, *With Congress and Cabinet* (Garden City, N.Y., 1924); Secretary of the Navy Josephus P. Daniels, *The Wilson Era*, 2 vols. (Chapel Hill, N.C., 1944–46); Secretary of the Treasury William G. McAdoo, *Crowded Years: The Reminiscences of William G. McAdoo* (Boston, 1931); and Committee on Public Information head George C. Creel, *Rebel at Large* (New York, 1947). Daniels's sometimes faulty memory should be checked against *The Cabinet Diaries of Josephus Daniels, 1913–1921*, ed. E. David Cronon (Lincoln, Neb., 1963). A selection from the correspondence of Wilson's secretary of the interior has been published in Anne W. Lane and Louise H. Wall, eds., *The Letters of Franklin K. Lane: Personal and Political* (Boston, 1922).

The first biographies of Wilson tended to be either eulogistic, such as Henry Jones Ford's campaign biography, *Woodrow Wilson, The Man and His Work: A Biographical Study* (New York, 1916) and William E. Dodd's hero-worshipping *Woodrow Wilson and His Work* (Garden City, N.Y., 1920), or bitterly hostile, such as Robert E. Annin's unflattering portrait of Wilson as an egotistical liar, *Woodrow Wilson: A Character Study* (New York, 1924). David Lawrence's *The True Story of Woodrow Wilson* (New York, 1924) was a friendly though not uncritical account based upon personal knowledge and interviews. But the first major breakthrough in Wilson scholarship came with the publication of Ray Stannard Baker's *Woodrow Wilson: Life and Letters*, 8 vols. (Garden City, N.Y., 1927–39). Baker, a writer for *McClure's* and *American Magazine* who had served as press bureau chief for the American delegation at the Paris Peace Conference, was picked by Wilson himself shortly before his death to be his biographer and was given access to the Wilson papers by Mrs. Wilson. Baker's final volume ends with Wilson's return from Paris, and his work is stronger on details than in interpretation. But his publication of extensive extracts from Wilson's personal papers and from correspondence and interviews with Wilson's relatives, friends, and associates made his eight volumes a major source for such later Wilson biographies as David Loth, *Woodrow Wilson: The Fifteenth Point* (Philadelphia, 1941), and Herbert C. F. Bell, *Woodrow Wilson and the People* (Garden City, N.Y., 1945).

The renewed interest in Wilson spurred by the Second World War and its aftermath coupled with the opening of the massive Wilson Papers in the Library of Congress have led to a revolution in Wilson scholarship since Baker's volumes. George C. Osborn has examined Wilson's life up to his election as president of Princeton University in his *Woodrow Wilson: The Early Years* (Baton Rouge, La., 1968), while Henry W. Bragdon has published *Woodrow Wilson: The Academic Years* (Cambridge, Mass., 1967). William Diamond, *The Economic Thought of Woodrow Wilson* (Baltimore, 1943), underlines the intellectual limitations of Wilson's progressivism and internationalism. Richard Hofstadter takes much the same approach in his sketch of Wilson in his *American Political Tradition and the Men Who Made It* (New York, 1948). John Morton Blum's *Woodrow Wilson and the Politics of Morality* (Boston, 1956) and John A. Garraty's *Woodrow Wilson: A Great Life in Brief* (New York, 1956) are brief, but perceptive, interpretive biographies. Alexander L. George and Juliette L. George, *Woodrow Wilson and Colonel House: A Personality Study* (New York, 1956), ascribe Wilson's "compulsive" yearning for power to a sense of inadequacy produced by an overly demanding father. Sigmund Freud and William C. Bullitt, *Thomas Woodrow Wilson, Twenty-eighth President of the United States: A Psychological Study* (Boston, 1967), is a less successful attempt at a psychoanalytical interpretation. The most comprehensive full-length biography is Arthur Walworth's generally adulatory *Woodrow Wilson,* 2 vols. (New York, 1948; 2nd revised one-volume edition, Boston, 1965).

But the preeminent Wilson biographer of the present generation is Arthur S. Link of Princeton University. Link's published work on Wilson includes the first five volumes of a projected nine-volume biography—*Wilson: The Road to the White House* (Princeton, 1947), *Wilson: The New Freedom* (Princeton, 1956), *Wilson: The Struggle for Neutrality, 1914–1915* (Princeton, 1960), *Wilson: Confusions and Crises, 1915–1916* (Princeton, 1964), and *Wilson: Campaigns for Progressivism and Peace, 1916–1917* (Princeton, 1965)— and *Woodrow Wilson and the Progressive Era, 1910–1917* (New York, 1954), in the New American Nation Series; *Wilson the Diplomatist* (Baltimore, 1957); *Woodrow Wilson: A Brief Biography* (Cleveland, 1963); and *The Higher Realism of Woodrow Wilson and Other Essays* (Nashville, 1971). At first Link was relatively detached, even critical, toward Wilson. Unfortunately, he has become increasingly eulogistic with time. Nevertheless, his work is indispensable for all students of the man and his times.

The celebration of the centennial year of Wilson's birth inspired the publication of a spate of commemorative and interpretive articles, most, as befitting the occasion, sympathetic to Wilson. The autumn 1956 issue of the *Virginia Quarterly Review* and the autumn 1956 and winter 1957 issues of *Confluence* were entirely devoted to Wilson. Other centennial year–inspired collections include: Em Bowles Alsop, ed., *The Greatness of Woodrow Wilson, 1856–1956* (New York, 1956); Victor S. Mamatey, ed., *Florida State University Studies, No. 23: Woodrow Wilson Centennial Issue* (Tallahassee, 1956); Edward H. Buehrig, ed., *Wilson's Foreign Policy in Perspective* (Bloomington, Ind., 1957); Arthur P. Dudden, ed., *Woodrow Wilson and the World of Today* (Philadelphia, 1957); and Earl Latham, ed., *The Philosophy and Politics of Woodrow Wilson* (Chicago, 1958).

There are regrettably few scholarly biographies of leading figures in the Wilson administration or of key Democratic congressional leaders. Paola E. Coletta has written a three-volume biography of William Jennings Bryan: *William Jennings Bryan*, Vol. I, *Political Evangelist, 1860–1908* (Lincoln, Neb., 1964), *William Jennings Bryan*, Vol. II, *Progressive Politican and Moral Statesman, 1909–1915* (Lincoln, Neb., 1969), and *William Jennings Bryan*, Vol. III, *Political Puritan, 1915–1925* (Lincoln, Neb., 1969). Lawrence W. Levine, *Defender of the Faith: William Jennings Bryan, the Last Decade, 1915–1925* (New York, 1965), is excellent on Bryan during the years after his resignation as secretary of state. John Morton Blum's *Joe Tumulty and the Wilson Era* (Boston, 1951) is a first-rate piece of work, as is Stanley Coben's *A. Mitchell Palmer: Politician* (New York, 1963). Alpheus T. Mason, *Brandeis: A Free Man's Life* (New York, 1946), is a full-scale biography of one of Wilson's most influential advisers; Melvin I. Urofsky, *A Mind of One Piece: Brandeis and American Reform* (New York, 1971), is more interpretive. Margaret L. Coit, *Mr. Baruch* (Boston, 1957), and Clarence H. Cramer, *Newton D. Baker* (Cleveland, 1961), are adequate biographies of their subjects.

Useful studies of Democratic congressional leaders are: Rixey Smith and Norman Beasley, *Carter Glass* (New York, 1939); A. M. Arnett, *Claude Kitchin and the Wilson War Politics* (Boston, 1937);

Dewey W. Grantham, Jr., *Hoke Smith and the Politics of the New South* (Baton Rouge, La., 1958); George C. Osborn, *John Sharp Williams: Planter-Statesman of the Deep South* (Baton Rouge, La., 1943); and Monroe L. Billington, *Thomas P. Gore: The Blind Senator from Oklahoma* (Lawrence, Kans., 1967).

Compared with the voluminous writings on Wilson's foreign policies, relatively little monographic work has been published on the domestic side of his administration. Dewey W. Grantham, Jr., "Southern Congressional Leaders and the New Freedom, 1913–1917," *Journal of Southern History,* XIII (1947), 439–459, and Richard J. Abrams, "Woodrow Wilson and the Southern Congressmen, 1913–1916," *Journal of Southern History,* XXII (1956), 417–437, examine the influence of southern congressmen upon Wilson's domestic policies. On Wilson and labor, see John S. Smith, "Organized Labor and Government in the Wilson Era, 1913–1921: Some Conclusions," *Labor History,* III (1962), 265–286; on Wilson and the Negro, Nancy J. Weiss, "The Negro and the New Freedom: Fighting Wilsonian Segregation," *Political Science Quarterly,* LXXXIV (1969), 61–79. Charles Forcey, *The Crossroads of Liberalism: Croly, Weyl, Lippmann, and the Progressive Era, 1900–1925* (New York, 1961), analyzes the attitude toward and influence upon Wilson of *The New Republic* group. Melvin I. Urofsky, *Big Steel and the Wilson Adiminstration: A Study in Business-Government Relations* (Columbus, Ohio, 1969), reveals the gap between Wilsonian rhetoric and practice on the trust question.

Frederic L. Paxson, *American Democracy and the World War, 3* vols. (Boston, 1936–48), remains the fullest account of the United States during World War I. But the student should also consult: Grosvenor Clark, *Industrial America in the World War* (Boston, 1923), Paul A. C. Koistinen, "The 'Industrial-Military Complex' in Historical Perspective: World War I," *Business History Review,* XLI (1967), 378–403, Daniel R. Beaver, *Newton D. Baker and the American War Effort, 1917–1919* (Lincoln, Neb., 1966), and K. Austin Kerr, *American Railroad Politics, 1914–1920* (Pittsburgh, 1968), on mobilization for war; Charles Gilbert, *American Financing of World War I* (Westport, Conn., 1970), on war financing; Seward W. Livermore, *Politics Is Adjourned: Woodrow Wilson and the War Congress, 1916–1918* (Middletown, Conn., 1966), on executive-congressional relations; James R. Mock and Cedric Larson, *Words That*

*Won the War: The Story of the Committee on Public Information,
1917–1919* (Princeton, 1939), on home-front propaganda activities;
and Zechariah Chafee, Jr., *Free Speech in the United States* (Cambridge, Mass., 1941), Horace C. Peterson and Gilbert Fite, *Opponents of War, 1917–1918* (Madison, Wis., 1957), Harry N. Scheiber,
The Wilson Administration and Civil Liberties, 1917–1921 (Ithaca,
N.Y., 1960), and Joan M. Jensen, *The Price of Vigilance* (Chicago,
1968), on civil liberties during wartime.

The two most useful accounts of the principles underlying Wilson's approach to foreign affairs are Harley Notter, *The Origins
of the Foreign Policy of Woodrow Wilson* (Baltimore, 1937), and
Link's *Wilson the Diplomatist.* Robert E. Osgood's *Ideals and Self-Interest in America's Foreign Relations* (Chicago, 1953) is critical of
Wilson's moralistic approach to foreign affairs.

There is no single comprehensive volume dealing overall with
Wilson's Latin American policy. The administration's Caribbean
policy is surveyed in Selig Adler, "Bryan and Wilsonian Caribbean
Penetration," *Hispanic-American Historical Review*, XX (1940),
198–226, and Dana G. Munro, *Intervention and Dollar Diplomacy
in the Caribbean, 1900–1921* (Princeton, 1964). George Baker, "The
Wilson Administration and Cuba, 1913–1921," *Mid-America*, XLVI
(1964), 48–74, studies United States–Cuban relations during those
years. Wilson's unhappy experiences with Mexico have been the
subject of extensive study: Robert E. Quirk, *An Affair of Honor:
Woodrow Wilson and the Occupation of Veracruz* (Lexington, Ky.,
1962); Clarence C. Clendenen, *The United States and Pancho Villa*
(Ithaca, N.Y., 1961); Kenneth J. Grieb, *The United States and
Huerta* (Lincoln, Neb., 1969); and P. Edward Haley, *Revolution
and Intervention: The Diplomacy of Taft and Wilson with Mexico,
1910–1917* (Cambridge, Mass., 1970).

A. Whitney Griswold, *The Far Eastern Policy of the United States*
(New Haven, 1938), is a general survey of United States–Far Eastern
relations. Two generally sympathetically pro-Wilson studies are
Tien-yi Li, *Woodrow Wilson and Far Eastern Policy, 1913–1917*
(Kansas City, Mo., 1952), and Roy W. Curry, *Woodrow Wilson and
Far Eastern Policy, 1913–1921* (New York, 1957). Burton F. Beers,
Vain Endeavor: Robert Lansing's Attempt to End the American-Japanese Rivalry (Durham, N.C., 1962), deals with the Lansing-Ishii agreement.

The most controversial aspect of Wilsonian foreign policy has been American neutrality policies during World War I. Given the disillusionment with the war that marked the 1920s and 1930s, writing upon the subject during those years was dominated by the so-called revisionist school. While their emphases differed, all agreed that American entry was a tragic mistake and all blamed Wilson's failure to follow truly neutral policies. C. Hartley Grattan's *Why We Fought* (New York, 1929) and Walter Millis's best-selling *Road to War: America, 1914–1917* (Boston, 1935) stress the role of propaganda and economic ties with the Allies; Edwin Borchard and W. P. Lage, in *Neutrality for the United States* (New Haven, 1937), and Alice M. Morrisey, in *The American Defense of Neutral Rights, 1914–1917* (Cambridge, Mass., 1939), accuse Wilson of failing to follow recognized rules of neutrality. The most thoroughly researched of the revisionist accounts is Charles C. Tansill's *America Goes to War* (Boston, 1938). A multiple-causationist, Tansill offers no single explanation for why the United States went to war, but his conviction that American entry was a mistake colors his work throughout.

Charles Seymour's *American Diplomacy During the World War* (Baltimore, 1934) is a sympathetic appraisal of Wilson's policies that ascribes American entry to Germany's resumption of unrestricted submarine warfare. But it was not until after the Second World War that the historiographical tide shifted strongly in Wilson's favor. Edward H. Buehrig, *Woodrow Wilson and the Balance of Power* (Bloomington, Ind., 1955), credits Wilson with a realistic grasp of national interests in his pro-British policies and later commitment to collective security. Daniel M. Smith's *The Great Departure: The United States and World War I* (New York, 1965) takes much the same approach, but overstates the importance of House and Lansing in shaping American policy. The most balanced and judicious of the newer pro-Wilson accounts is Ernest R. May, *The World War and American Isolation, 1914–1917* (Cambridge, Mass., 1959). Based upon impressive multiarchival research, May's work places the diplomatic controversies of the war period in the context of domestic politics within the United States, Britain, and Germany.

A growing number of monographs illuminate specific aspects of the background of American involvement. Daniel M. Smith, *Robert Lansing and American Neutrality, 1914–1917* (Berkeley, 1958), is an admiring portrait that exaggerates Lansing's importance. Ross Gregory, *Walter Hines Page: Ambassador to the Court of St. James's* (Lexington, Ky., 1970), is a study of the role of the strongly pro-Allied American ambassador to Britain. Karl E. Birnbaum, *Peace Moves and U-Boat Warfare* (Stockholm, 1958), traces the evolution of German policy toward the United States. Armin Rappaport's *The British Press and Wilsonian Neutrality* (Stanford, Cal., 1951) examines British newspaper and magazine opinion on Wilson's policies. H. C. Peterson, *Propaganda for War: The Campaign Against American Neutrality, 1914–1917* (Norman, Okla., 1939), overstates the influence of British propaganda. Samuel R. Spencer, Jr., *Decision for War, 1917* (Rindge, N.H., 1953) and Barbara W. Tuchman, *The Zimmermann Telegram* (New York, 1958), focus on the last stage before the American declaration of war.

As for wartime diplomacy, Thomas A. Bailey covers United States relations with the remaining neutrals in *The Policy of the United States Toward the Neutrals, 1917–1918* (Baltimore, 1942), while David F. Trask has studied inter-Allied relations in *The United States in the Supreme War Council* (Middletown, Conn., 1961). The American military role is described in Edward M. Coffman, *The War to End All Wars: The American Military Experience in World War I* (New York, 1968), and Harvey A. DeWeerd, *President Wilson Fights His War: World War I and American Intervention* (New York, 1968). Louis L. Gerson's *Woodrow Wilson and the Rebirth of Poland* (New Haven, 1953) shows the role of the Polish-Americans in shaping Wilson's Polish policy, while Victor S. Mamatey, *The United States and East Central Europe, 1914–1918* (Princeton, 1957), traces the development of Wilson's policy toward the Hapsburg Empire. Betty Miller Unterberger, *America's Siberian Expedition, 1918–1920* (Durham, N.C., 1956), ascribes the intervention in Russia to Wilson's fear of Japanese expansionism; George F. Kennan's *Soviet-American Relations, 1917–1920*, Vol. I, *Russia Leaves the War* (Princeton, 1956), and Vol. II, *The Decision to Intervene* (Princeton, 1958), is a more comprehensive treatment of United States policy toward the Bolshevik regime.

The background of the League of Nations idea is traced by Ruhl J. Bartlett, *The League to Enforce Peace* (Chapel Hill, N.C., 1944), and Warren F. Kuehl, *Seeking World Order: The United States and World Organization to 1920* (Nashville, 1969). Laurence W.

Martin's *Peace Without Victory: Woodrow Wilson and the British Liberals* (New Haven, 1958) shows the influence of British liberals in shaping Wilson's peace program, while Arno J. Mayer's *Political Origins of the New Diplomacy* (New Haven, 1959) stresses the importance of the Bolshevik challenge. N. Gordon Levin, Jr., *Woodrow Wilson and World Politics: America's Response to War and Revolution* (New York, 1968), sees Wilson as motivated by the desire to establish a stable liberal-capitalist world order safe from the threat of imperialism on the right and revolution on the left.

H. W. V. Temperley, ed., *A History of the Peace Conference of Paris*, 6 vols. (London, 1920–24), remains the most detailed account of the peace conference, but has been rendered largely out-of-date by more recent scholarship drawing upon archival materials not then available. Ray Stannard Baker's *Woodrow Wilson and the World Settlement*, 3 vols. (Garden City, N.Y., 1922) is a pro-Wilson account based on Baker's personal notebooks kept while he was press chief for the American delegation, on Wilson's own peace conference files, and on an extensive correspondence with participants. Two accounts critical of Wilson by participants are John Maynard Keynes, *The Economic Consequences of the Peace* (New York, 1920), and Harold Nicolson, *Peacemaking, 1919* (Boston, 1933). Paul M. Birdsall's *Versailles Twenty Years After* (New York, 1941) praises Wilson's statesmanship at Paris and credits him with having attained his major peace aims. Thomas A. Bailey, *Woodrow Wilson and the Lost Peace* (New York, 1944), is more critical of Wilson's inflexibility, errors in judgment, and inconsistencies, but lauds his devotion to his ideals, acknowledges his success in improving the treaty, and concludes that he secured fulfillment of most of his Fourteen Points.

There is a large body of monographic literature dealing with different aspects of the peace conference. Lawrence E. Gelfand, *The Inquiry: American Preparations for Peace, 1917–1919* (New Haven, 1963), analyzes the role of the scholars assembled under the direction of Colonel House to plan for the conference, while Seth P. Tillman, *Anglo-American Relations at the Paris Peace Conference of 1919* (Princeton, 1961), reveals the basic harmony between American and British aims. The contributors to Joseph P. O'Grady, ed., *The Immigrants' Influence on Wilson's Peace Policies* (Lexington, Ky., 1967), assess the influence of different American ethnic groups upon Wilson. David F. Trask, *General Tasker Howard Bliss and the "Ses-*

sions of the World," 1919 (Philadelphia, 1966), appraises Bliss's role at the conference. Louis A. R. Yates, *The United States and French Security* (New York, 1957), examines the American response to French demands for security. The Shantung question is dealt with in Russell H. Fifield, *Woodrow Wilson and the Far East: The Diplomacy of the Shantung Question* (New York, 1952). On the drafting of the League covenant, see David Hunter Miller, *My Diary at the Conference of Paris,* 21 vols. (New York, 1924), and *The Drafting of the Covenant,* 2 vols. (New York, 1928); on the reparations issue, see Philip M. Burnett, *Reparations at the Paris Peace Conference from the Standpoint of the American Delegation,* 2 vols. (Cambridge, Mass., 1940). Arno J. Mayer's *Politics and Diplomacy of Peacemaking: Containment and Counterrevolution at Versailles, 1918–1919* (New York, 1967) sees fear of and hostility toward Bolshevik Russia the dominating concern of the peacemakers; John M. Thompson, *Russia, Bolshevism, and the Versailles Treaty* (Princeton, 1966), is a more balanced account of the Bolshevik question at Paris. Studies of individual nations and the treaty include: René Albrecht-Carrie, *Italy at the Paris Peace Conference* (New York, 1938); Alma Lukau, *The German Delegation at the Paris Peace* (New York, 1941); Sherman D. Spector, *Rumania at the Paris Peace Conference* (New York, 1962); Ivo J. Lederer, *Yugoslavia at the Paris Peace Conference* (New Haven, 1963); and Laurence Evans, *The United States and the Partition of Turkey, 1914–1923* (Baltimore, 1967).

W. Stull Holt, *Treaties Defeated by the Senate* (Baltimore, 1933), and D. F. Fleming, *The United States and the League of Nations* (New York, 1932), review the Senate battle over ratification of the treaty. Selig Adler, *The Isolationist Impulse: Its Twentieth Century Reaction* (New York, 1957), stresses the importance of liberal defections and the psychological unpreparedness of the majority of the American people to accept collective security. Thomas A. Bailey's *Woodrow Wilson and the Great Betrayal* (New York, 1945) blames the defeat of the treaty upon Wilson's adamant refusal to compromise. Kurt Wimer has examined aspects of Wilson's own strategy in four articles: "Woodrow Wilson's Plan to Enter the League of Nations through an Executive Agreement," *Western Political Quarterly,* XI (1958), 800–812; "Woodrow Wilson's Plan for a Vote of Confidence," *Pennsylvania History,* XXVIII (1961), 279–293;

"Woodrow Wilson and a Third Nomination," *Pennsylvania History*, XXIX (1962), 193–211; and "Woodrow Wilson Tries Conciliation: An Effort That Failed," *The Historian*, XXV (1963), 419–438. John A. Garraty's *Henry Cabot Lodge: A Biography* (New York, 1953) illuminates the role of the Massachusetts senator. Ralph Stone, *The Irreconcilables: The Fight Against the League of Nations* (Lexington, Ky., 1970), is excellent on the Senate bitter-enders.

Apart from the Paris Peace Conference and the fight over the treaty, there has been little scholarly work done on the postarmistice years of the Wilson administration. A number of monographs deal with the Red Scare: Robert K. Murray, *Red Scare: A Study in National Hysteria, 1919–1920* (Minneapolis, 1955); William Preston, Jr., *Aliens and Dissenters: Federal Suppression of Radicals, 1903–1933* (Cambridge, Mass., 1963); and Stanley Coben, "A Study in Nativism: The American Red Scare of 1919–1920," *Political Science Quarterly*, LXXIX (1964), 52–75, and his biography of A. Mitchell Palmer. James R. Mock and Evangeline Thurber, *Report on Demobilization* (Norman, Okla., 1944), reviews the postwar demobilization process; John D. Hicks, *Rehearsal for Disaster: The Boom and Collapse of 1919–1920* (Gainesville, Fla., 1961), is more critical of Wilson's lack of leadership on the domestic front. Daniel M. Smith, "Lansing and the Wilson Interregnum, 1919–1920," *The Historian*, XXI (1959), 135–161, describes Lansing's bid to fill the vacuum left by Wilson's illness. David M. Burner, *The Politics of Provincialism: The Democratic Party in Transition, 1918–1932* (New York, 1968), traces the break-up of the Wilson coalition, while Wesley Bagby, *The Road to Normalcy: The Presidential Campaign and Election of 1920* (Baltimore, 1962), is excellent on the 1920 election. Daniel M. Smith, *Aftermath of War: Bainbridge Colby and Wilsonian Diplomacy, 1920–1921* (Philadelphia, 1970), is informative on postarmistice diplomacy. Gene Smith's *When the Cheering Stopped: The Last Years of Woodrow Wilson* (New York, 1964) is a journalistic account covering the period from Wilson's breakdown during his speaking tour in behalf of the League to his death.

Index